Appalachian Fertility Decline

Appalachian

A Demographic and

UNIVERSITY OF KENTUCKY

Gordon F. De Jong

Fertility Decline

Sociological Analysis

PRESS · LEXINGTON · 1968

*To my mother and
the memory of my father,
who introduced me to Appalachia*

Foreword

Chinese scholars more than 2,500 years ago recognized that an excess population in relation to land resources in an agricultural economy resulted in poverty. Their recommended solution to eliminate poverty resulting from an excess population was to have the government move people from overpopulated to underpopulated areas. The proposed solution was not entirely satisfactory, for it failed to take into account how quickly depletions through migration can be restored through natural increase when birth rates remain substantially higher than death rates.

With a current world population of 3.3 billion projected to exceed 7 billion by the end of the century, the concern about problems of overpopulation is perhaps greater than at any previous period, including the era of controversy generated by Malthus' famous essay on the principle of population, which first appeared in 1798. Now it is widely recognized that neither migration nor economic revolution (as the Marxists long maintained) offers more than temporary respite from the Malthusian specter. Ultimately natural increase must be brought under control, either by limiting the birth rate or by increasing the death rate. And though we may inadvertently take the latter route, the former is the more acceptable choice.

Within this setting Gordon De Jong's study of fertility decline in the Southern Appalachian Region assumes considerable importance. In recent years Appalachia has attracted fresh attention as one of the major areas of poverty in a generally affluent society, and one of the major causes of its poverty has been identified as the imbalance of population and economic resources. Indeed, increasing population pressure as a source of the basic problems was highlighted more than thirty years ago by the authors of the United

States Department of Agriculture publication *Economic and Social Problems and Conditions of the Southern Appalachians.* Since for many decades the region had been consistently losing population through migration, it was evident that the sustained population increase stemmed from high fertility.

In 1962 the findings of a second general survey of the region were published in the volume *The Southern Appalachian Region: A Survey.* Professor John Belcher, who studied the population changes within the region as part of the survey, at that time called attention to a major decline in regional birth rates during the 1950-1960 decade. The finding was unexpected in view of the history of the region, the fact that its population was still predominantly rural, and the continued rise of relatively high post-World War II national fertility rates through 1957. This anomaly attracted the interest of De Jong, who then undertook an investigation of the reasons for the decline of fertility in Appalachia.

His findings, reported in this volume, exemplify the approach of the social demographer, who draws his theory and techniques from the disciplines of both sociology and demography. As a demographer, De Jong has identified the heavy out-migration from the region, which is highly selective of young adults, as the most plausible reason for fertility decline. Although migration had an important influence, he found that at most only 20 percent of the variation in the changes in county fertility rates was associated with migration losses. Drawing upon his sociological knowledge, he then made an ingenious application of data from a regional attitude survey to determine if attitudes, beliefs, and values were associated with fertility changes. On the basis of his careful analysis he concluded that the data provide consistent evidence that these cultural factors were closely associated with the observed changes in reproduction patterns.

The significance of De Jong's findings is not so much that cultural factors are related to reproductive behavior but that underlying values and beliefs that support high fertility are subject to relatively rapid change under certain circumstances. The circumstances that bring about these changes remain to be fully explored in the developing of a strategy for population control that will prove more effective than current frontal assaults that are often resisted by cultural barriers. As an initial effort, however, De Jong's findings offer encouragement to those who seek to solve the related problems of over-population and poverty, not only in the United States but throughout the world.

THOMAS R. FORD
Lexington, Kentucky
January, 1968

Preface

It has been more than two years since this study was completed. During this time two significant trends have developed that relate to the topic. First, a number of events have increased public awareness of the links between population growth and social and economic problems of society. The population-resources debate on the world level is no more significant in this regard than are the high fertility-poverty discussions on the national level. Second, the amount of money allocated to federal area-development programs in economically depressed areas of the United States, such as Appalachia, has been reduced—at a time when the links between such rural and urban problems as poverty, low education, poor housing, and restricted occupational opportunities would seem to dictate greater rather than smaller allocations of national resources.

My purpose in the study was to describe an important population trend in Appalachia—the decline in the birth rate—and to analyze some possible explanations for the change. Attaining this purpose, however, defied narrow investigative confines, and consequently, this study attempted to incorporate both demographic and sociological perspectives. The inclusion of these perspectives touched some significant issues for population theory and research, as well as for the future of the Southern Appalachians.

The study was made possible by several grants. The attitude data on fertility and family planning were collected as part of a larger study of the Southern Appalachians financed by the Ford Foundation. The Central Fund for Research of The Pennsylvania State University and the Council of the Southern Mountains provided grants to assist in the analysis and report phases of the study.

The work was started while I was at the University of

Kentucky and completed after I joined the faculty of The Pennsylvania State University. I am indebted to several administrators, including A. Lee Coleman, M. E. John, Paul T. Baker, and Donald P. Kent for their interest and for being cognizant of the value of that commodity, time. The statistical analysis was greatly facilitated by the cooperation of personnel of The Pennsylvania State University and the University of Kentucky computer centers.

Parts of chapters two and three were previously published in *Social Forces*, XLIII (October 1963), pages 89-96. I am grateful to the editors for their permission to reprint the material.

Along the way I had the benefit of the insights of several trusted mentors and colleagues. Debts are owed to Donald J. Bogue, C. Michael Lanphier, James H. Copp, C. Milton Coughenour, James S. Brown, James W. Gladden, and George Lauber, Jr. Particular gratitude is extended to George A. Hillery, Jr., and Thomas R. Ford, who gave perceptive and patient attention to earlier versions of the manuscript. Their criticisms were invaluable. The shortcomings are mine.

Finally, to my wife, Caroline, for editorial assistance, encouragement, and understanding, I express my deepest thanks.

GORDON F. DE JONG
University Park, Pennsylvania
New Year's Day, 1968

Contents

Foreword   vii

Preface   xi

Introduction   1

1. Characteristics of the Population   9

2. Fertility Patterns   31

3. Migration and Residence Patterns   52

4. Attitudes   70

5. Personal and Social Characteristics and Attitudes   88

6. Toward Theory and Application   101

Appendix A. Fertility Data for Southern
Appalachian Region Counties, 1930–1960   109

Appendix B. Source of Data   133

Index   135

Figures

1. *The Region as Defined in 1960*   19-20

2. *Population Growth of the Southern Appalachian Region and the United States, 1900–1960*   21

3. *Distribution of Families by Amount of 1959 Income, by Percentage, for the Southern Appalachian Region and the United States*   22

4. *General Fertility Rates, 1930*   39-40

5. *General Fertility Rates, 1960*   41-42

6. *Low Fertility Counties, 1950*   42-44

7. *Low Fertility Counties, 1960*   45-46

Introduction

Appalachia—once a region about which most Americans knew very little and probably cared even less—is an area both graced by the beauties of nature and scourged by the often unsuccessful efforts of men to make an acceptable livelihood: An area with an ample supply of some resources that either are not in great demand or no longer need a large labor force for their production: An area where live people with a proud heritage of individualism and private industry but where many now rely on private and government aid to help make life at all tolerable.

But Appalachia is no longer unknown to Americans. The problems of this "other America" are frequent topics for news articles, television documentaries, political debates, and editorials. It is not that the problems of the area are unique or different from those of other so-called depressed areas. Rather, it is the severity of the problems, combined with numerous circumstantial factors, that have tended to focus public attention on the area. Whatever the reason, the increased awareness of Appalachian problems has quickened interest not only in developing corrective programs but also, as a prior step, in obtaining basic descriptions and analyzing social trends. From these data emerge a general body of factors that contribute to an understanding and a prediction of the causes and correlates of problem areas.

Most observations and investigations of Appalachian problems have emphasized economic factors. In fact, some investigators refer to the area in the same terms that they use to describe underdeveloped countries. A theme of Harry Caudill's book *Night Comes to the Cumberlands* is that the area has been the victim of outside exploiters who have plundered its resources.

An example of this concentration on resources is the

emphasis given to the rise and fall of the coal industry, which had been the major source of wealth and employment in much of Appalachia. The increased use of petroleum products for fuel is one reason for the decline. Another factor is the advent of automation, which has eliminated thousands of jobs in the once-bustling coalfields. An inevitable result has been the unemployed and sometimes even the unemployable worker. Can new industry be found to replace the old, or can massive public programs be instituted to provide employment for these people? These questions are raised continually. Meanwhile, many people are ill-housed, ill-educated, and ill-fed.

Unmistakably, economic issues are of immediate importance in the problems of Appalachia. They are not the only ones, however, and they are related to other important factors. Economic issues probably would be less important if the area had a smaller population. Low income, substandard housing, and poor education are part of the depressed-area syndrome of difficulties—difficulties that are traceable largely to an imbalance of population and resources. In this light an investigation of Appalachian population trends offers added perspective to the area's frequently discussed problems.

Notwithstanding, this study does not use primarily a problem-solving approach but is directed toward answering theoretically significant questions about population trends. In answering these questions, however, it frequently gives insights into problem solving.

Population trends have their genesis in three components: births, deaths, and migration. Prior research identifies births and migration as the variables of prime significance in understanding recent population trends in Appalachia.[1] This research concentrates on births and factors associated with differential birth rates. The specific focus is on factors associated

[1] See, for example, John C. Belcher, "Population Growth and Characteristics"; James S. Brown and George A. Hillery, Jr., "The Great Migration, 1940-1960"; and C. Horace Hamilton, "Health and Health Services"—all in Thomas R. Ford, ed., *The Southern Appalachian Region: A Survey* (Lexington: University of Kentucky Press, 1962), 37-53, 54-78, 219-44 (hereafter this volume cited as *SAR*).

with the decline of fertility for the white population living in the Southern Appalachian Region.[2]

Perhaps the nature of the problem can best be defined by an explanation of how the study developed. The people of Southern Appalachia have had one of the highest reproduction rates of any major region of the United States during the past century. Preliminary data from the 1950–1960 decade indicated, however, that birth rates in the region had dropped. As a consequence of the declining fertility and net migration loss, the population decreased between 1950 and 1960 for the first time since census data have become available. The question that naturally follows is what factors affected this decline?

There are several reasons for initiating a study of Appalachian fertility. One, reflecting a theoretical interest, concerns the application of both sociological and demographic theory to an essentially demographic problem in an effort to determine what factors are important in understanding a given population phenomenon. This is directly related to the frequent criticism that demographers have neglected theory and the retort that sociologists have offered theoretical explanations with little empirical reference. There is probably some truth in both positions. A major difficulty in the clarification of this issue is the meaning of the term "theory." However, admitting the vagueness that exists, researchers must recognize the value in the critics' statements and then pursue particular problems with all the conceptual and empirical tools available.

A second level of interest, with considerable theoretical and applied reference, is the focus on fertility as a critical component of population growth. The attention allotted to fertility (particularly high fertility) in popular literature and scientific writings often reflects the concern that the pessimistic Malthusian thesis may become a reality. The dynamics of population growth are pinpointed by the "demographic theory

---

[2] This study was limited to the white population to avoid the complications that would be introduced by the inclusion of the nonwhite population, which, although constituting only about 6 percent of the total population, is highly concentrated in the metropolitan areas.

of transition" which, despite its empirical and logical weaknesses, vividly portrays the relationship between births and deaths that produces extreme population growth—a high fertility rate and a low death rate.

The continuation of a high fertility rate is of particular concern in relation to the world's underdeveloped countries. Puerto Rico is an example. At the beginning of the twentieth century the annual rate of births in Puerto Rico was about 40 per 1,000 population, and the annual rate of deaths was about 25 per 1,000. This resulted in a relatively modest rate of population increase. Only in the post-World War II era did the crude birth rate begin to decline, dropping to 35.9 in 1952. During the same period, however, the crude death rate declined to 9.2. As a consequence, the population increased very rapidly, even though there was considerable emigration. Many other nations including Mexico, Jamaica, Formosa, and Ceylon have exhibited similar trends.[3] The same type of relationship between births and deaths, along with heavy migration from the region, also has characterized the Southern Appalachian Region.

Much of the research into sociological and social psychological factors that affect fertility trends stems from the findings of the Indianapolis study.[4] This was the first study that systematically tested a number of social psychological hypotheses about fertility and family planning. However, a frequent criticism of the study concerns its restricted sample, which included only native-born white Protestants who had at least an eighth-grade education and had always resided in that city. The Princeton study of family growth was restricted to couples who had two children and who lived in seven Standard Metropolitan Statistical Areas of two million persons or more.[5] The present study, using data from the

[3] J. Mayone Stycos, *Family and Fertility in Puerto Rico* (New York: Columbia University Press, 1955), 6.

[4] Pascal K. Whelpton and Clyde V. Kiser, eds., *Social and Psychological Factors Affecting Fertility* (5 vols., New York: Milbank Memorial Fund, 1946-1958).

[5] Charles F. Westoff, Robert G. Potter, Jr., Philip C. Sagi, and Elliot G. Mishler, *Family Growth in Metropolitan America* (Princeton: Princeton University Press, 1961).

large, predominantly rural Southern Appalachian Region adds a different dimension to United States fertility data. Only the nonwhite population, which constitutes less than 6 percent of the region's population, is excluded from consideration.

Another reason underlying the choice of the region for this analysis is an interest in the people and problems of Appalachia and the social and demographic factors that influence the situation. An analysis of fertility is crucial to an understanding of significant changes in Southern Appalachia.

It would be helpful if there were a systematic theory that could serve as a basis for empirical research on the decline of fertility. However, a careful review of the literature on fertility reveals that no such theoretical structure has been developed. Other researchers, notably the Princeton research team, have come to the same conclusion. They summarize the current state of fertility theory as follows:

"A criticism directed frequently toward the Indianapolis Study has been that the hypotheses were generated in an unsystematic *ad hoc* fashion and were unintegrated. If one accepts the assumption that a single systematic theory existed whose utilization would have provided more fruitful hypotheses, the criticism would be valid. This alleged shortcoming of the Indianapolis Study formulation was foremost in the minds of the individuals concerned with the development of the new study, and much time and energy was consumed during the first year of the project in the search for a unified body of thought that could serve as the source of hypotheses. It soon became apparent, however, that there existed no single sociological or psychological theory that would encompass all the factors relevant to fertility. The reasons for this are many. First, and perhaps most significant, is the fact that research into the social and psychological factors affecting fertility is still at a stage where the primary needs are for gaining more information. When a body of empirically established relationships is secured from research guided by whatever unsystematic hunches and insights occur, then the development of a theory will be much more meaningful and useful.

"Secondly, the level of fertility is a complex result of many events. The antecedents to these events can be approached from the perspectives of several sciences, and even excluding the biological sciences, there remains the wide diversity of orientations represented among the behavioral disciplines of sociology, social psychology, and psychology. Moreover, even among the systematic theories extant in the literature relevant to our interest, the perspectives or interpretive models are not reducible one to the other nor are they wholly independent. The only recourse seemed to be to select and combine them, developing general hypotheses in the process."[6]

In the absence of a broad theoretical framework to encompass not only sociological and social psychological factors but also demographic factors, this study uses an alternative approach that emphasizes the testing of more basic propositions. The reasoning is that any theory of fertility change eventually will have to account for a wide range of data, and explorations from an inductive base will provide the best foundation. Unfortunately, an inductively oriented approach frequently is criticized as offering an eclectic treatment of a problem. Indeed, a wide range of factors may be related to fertility changes in the Southern Appalachians. In an effort to avoid this criticism the choice of crucial variables in this analysis was based largely on insights from the substantial accumulation of data in fertility studies.[7]

An encompassing thesis that fertility decline in the Southern Appalachian Region is associated with both demographic and sociologic variables is proposed. The demographic variable of prime importance is net migration, which in recent years has been primarily a net migration from the region. Sociological variables included in the investigation are residential patterns, socioeconomic status and attitude responses.

[6] *Ibid.*, 7-8.

[7] In particular, see "The Sociology of Human Fertility," *Current Sociology*, X (1961) and XI (1962); Ronald Freedman, Pascal K. Whelpton, Arthur A. Campbell, *Family Planning, Sterility, and Population Growth* (New York: McGraw-Hill, 1959); Pascal K. Whelpton, Arthur A. Campbell, and John E. Patterson, *Fertility and Family Planning in the United States* (Princeton: Princeton University Press, 1966); and Belcher, "Population Growth," *SAR*, 37-53.

The proposed interrelationship of the variables can be diagramed:

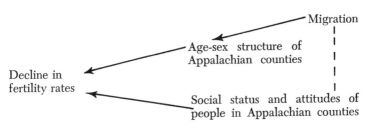

It is hypothesized that a major influence of migration on fertility rates occurs through the alteration of the age-sex structure in the Appalachian counties. Solid lines in the upper part of the diagram show this line of influence. The variables involved—fertility, migration, and the age-sex structure—are parts of the basic demographic system of any geographic unit.

Social status and attitude characteristics are additional factors that are frequently depicted as components of the social aggregate system of an area's population. Rural-urban distribution, socioeconomic status, and statements of attitudes about fertility of people living in different parts of Appalachia are among the kinds of factors to be considered. Interpreting attitudinal data in the context of social aggregate rather than social interaction systems (such as the family) is consistent with the treatment in the overwhelming majority of social demographic studies which report findings based on a sample survey of sociologically unrelated individuals. This approach to social psychological factors is not fundamentally different from that used in other aggregate studies, and the conclusions of this study are interpreted within the context of an aggregate system.

The broken line in the diagram demonstrates another possible way that these variables may influence fertility. Migration not only alters the age structure through selectivity of those who move, but it also is a means of changing the attitudes and values of the migrants. Although the Southern Appalachian Region has been characterized by heavy net migration losses during the past two decades, the region has had a sizable influx of people, as Brown and Hillery show.[8] Some of these individuals undoubtedly are an integral part of one or more Appalachian migration systems.[9] Some people make frequent moves from and then back to the region.[10] To an extent the migrants have contact with different attitudes and values held by people outside the area. Other residents, while not leaving the region, possibly are influenced through contacts with friends and family members who live elsewhere. It is reasonable to hypothesize that the traditional large-family orientation held by many residents of the Southern Appalachian Region has been affected by either direct or indirect contact with the normative structure of groups living outside the region. Unfortunately, data are not available to test this hypothesis.

Subsequent chapters will explore important recent demographic trends and characteristics of the region's population, comparing this data to the national characteristics. The study will explore the 1930–1960 trends in fertility rates in Appalachian counties, the effects of net migration on changes in the birth rate and the number of births in Appalachia, the rural-urban differences in fertility, and the relationship between fertility change and attitudes about fertility. Some implications of this study for demographic research, as well as for economic and social development in the Southern Appalachians, will be discussed.

[8] Brown and Hillery, "The Great Migration," *SAR*, 66-67.

[9] George A. Hillery, Jr., James S. Brown, and Gordon F. De Jong, "Migration Systems of the Southern Appalachians: Some Demographic Observations," *Rural Sociology*, XXX (March 1965), 31-48.

[10] James S. Brown, Harry K. Schwarzweller, and Joseph J. Mangalam, "Kentucky Mountain Migration and the Stem-family: An American Variation on a Theme by Le Play," *Rural Sociology*, XXVIII (March 1963), 48-69.

1. Characteristics of the Population

Appalachia is a highland area diagonally crossing the eastern part of the United States, but the agreement about its exact boundaries seems to end at this. The southern extremity of the area is usually considered to be the northern parts of Alabama and Georgia. Some definitions extend the northern border to encompass parts of New York, and others include a much smaller area.

The focus here is on the core areas of Appalachia. The area as defined in the recent Southern Appalachian Region survey included 190 counties and more than 80,000 square miles in Kentucky, Tennessee, West Virginia, Virginia, North Carolina, Alabama, and Georgia (Fig. 1, pp. 19-20)[1]—more than 600 miles long and 250 miles across at its widest point.

This definition of the Southern Appalachian Region is based on the concept of state economic areas as developed by the U.S. Bureau of the Census and the U.S. Department of Agriculture. Counties in which the livelihood is drawn from a similar economic base are grouped to form economic areas. Some areas are agricultural, and some are dominated by mining. Others are metropolitan areas containing a city of at least 50,000 people and the counties integrated with the central city.[2]

Three distinctive physiographic features mark the region. The Blue Ridge, the Great Smoky, and the Black mountains form the eastern edge of the region. Next comes the Great Valley, which is actually a series of valleys located primarily in Tennessee and Virginia. The western rim consists of the Cumberland and Allegheny plateaus.

A relatively small part of the region is truly mountainous with heavy forest covers and scant population. A large part can best be described as plateau area or hill land, and this area contains a sizable proportion of the region's population. The valley areas generally contain the most desirable agricultural land and most of the region's industry.

Within the confines of these general regional boundaries reside more than five and three-quarter million people, who often are victims of stereotyped and distorted images perpetuated by discussions of social and economic problems that focus on Appalachia. A more balanced view of the characteristics of Appalachian society and an awareness of the major social and economic changes in recent years can be gained by analyzing demographic data. An accurate picture of Appalachian population structure is basic not only for recognizing many of the social factors affecting fertility change but also for understanding the broader issue of the interaction between the demographic structure and process of a society and its social and economic structure and process. When the nature of this relationship is empirically determined, the potentiality of sociodemographic inferences from one set of phenomena to the other will become more of a reality.

POPULATION GROWTH

The most striking feature of the population trend of the region is the decline recorded during the 1950–1960 decade. Prior to 1950 the region had a steady increase in population that roughly paralleled the nation's growth (Fig. 2, p. 21). Between 1850 and 1950 the region's population grew from 1,892,948 to 5,833,263—a more than threefold increase.[3]

The 1960 census data show that the population change for the ten-year period since 1950 was different from national trends. While the nation's population increased more than 18 percent, the Southern Appalachian Region's population decreased by 2.8 percent, or about 160,000 persons (Table 1). This was the first time since census data have been available that the population of the region had not increased.

Variations from the national growth trends can be noted

[1] Rupert B. Vance, "The Region: A New Survey," *SAR*, 3.
[2] *Ibid.*, 3-4.
[3] John C. Belcher, "Population Growth and Characteristics," *SAR*, 39.

TABLE 1

Percentage Increase in Population between Censuses for the Southern Appalachian Region and the United States, 1900 to 1960

Area	1900-1910	1910-1920	1920-1930	1930-1940	1940-1950	1950-1960
Southern Appalachians	18.5	15.7	17.4	13.4	7.8	−2.8
United States	21.0	15.0	16.2	7.3	14.5	18.5

SOURCES: Compiled from *U.S. Census of Population, 1960*, and James S. Brown, Basic Population Data for the Southern Appalachians, University of Kentucky Social Research Service, 1958.

starting with the 1930 decade (Table 1). The depression years were ones of population growth in the Appalachians. Jobs were difficult to obtain in the industrial centers outside the region. The result was a slowing down of out-migration and an increase in population that exceeded the national average. During World War II the opportunities for employment outside the area were vastly increased, and out-migration increased accordingly. One consequence of the greater out-migration was a decline in the rate of the region's population increase from 13.4 percent between 1930 and 1940 to only 7.8 percent between 1940 and 1950. The percentage increase might have been even lower had it not been for the tremendous postwar "baby boom."[4] Nevertheless, the trend toward a lower rate of population increase was apparent.

As would be expected, not all counties in the Appalachians had a population decrease between 1950 and 1960. Returning to the three major physiographic divisions mentioned earlier the most striking change is the large population decline in the plateau areas on the western edge of the region (minus 11.6 percent). The Cumberland and Allegheny plateaus encompass much of Eastern Kentucky and parts of West Virginia, where the coalfields are located. The recent revolutions in mining techniques and the growing competition from other fuels have forced a tremendous decline in

[4] *Ibid.*, 50.

Appalachian Fertility Decline

TABLE 2

Percentage Distribution of the Rural Farm, Rural Nonfarm, and Urban Population of the Southern Appalachian Region and the United States, 1960

Area	Southern Appalachians	United States
Rural Farm	13.2	7.5
Rural Nonfarm	53.3	22.6
Urban	33.5	69.9

SOURCES: Compiled from *U.S. Census of Population, 1960*, and James S. Brown, Basic Population Data for the Southern Appalachians, University of Kentucky Social Research Service, 1958.

employment in the coal regions. Consequently, thousands of persons have migrated to northern cities in search of employment.

The population in the Blue Ridge Mountain area on the eastern rim of the region showed little change during the 1950 decade (minus 0.5 percent). Here the development of tourism and industry probably helped reduce the flow of out-migration.

In contrast to the plateau and mountain areas the Great Valley had a 7.4 percent increase in population between 1950 and 1960. The reasons for the increase may be numerous, but the two most prominent are the several cities and better grade of farm land. The influence of urbanization, although lagging about fifty years behind the national trend, is nevertheless becoming more important in the Appalachians.[5] The urban population increased more than 9 percent during the 1950s compared to the total population decline of nearly 3 percent. Still, the region's population is overwhelmingly rural, and the nation is predominantly urban (Table 2). Two out of three Appalachian residents were classed as rural by the 1960 census, compared to less than one resident in three in the nation. Rural-urban residence is an important factor in analyzing changing fertility patterns in the Southern Appalachians.

[5] Rupert B. Vance and Nicholas J. Demerath, *The Urban South* (Chapel Hill: University of North Carolina Press, 1954), 33.

AGE AND RACIAL COMPOSITION

The Appalachian population not only deviates from the national average in growth trends and population distribution but also in composition features. Two of the basic composition features are race and age. The composition of the population and changes that occurred between 1950 and 1960 are of immediate relevance in understanding changes in Appalachian fertility.

The term "color" as used in the United States Census refers to a division of the population into two groups, white and nonwhite. In the Southern Appalachians, more than 99 percent of those classed as nonwhite are Negroes.

TABLE 3

Percentage Distribution of the White and Nonwhite Population of the Southern Appalachian Region and the United States, 1960

Area	White	Nonwhite
Southern Appalachians	94.4	5.6
United States	88.6	11.4

SOURCES: Compiled from *U.S. Census of Population, 1960*, and James S. Brown, Basic Population Data for the Southern Appalachians, University of Kentucky Social Research Service, 1958.

Compared to the nation, Appalachia has a much smaller proportion of nonwhite population (Table 3). In 1960 the percentage was only about one-half that of the national population (5.6 percent compared to 11.4 percent, respectively), and most Appalachian nonwhites lived in or near a metropolitan center. A notable exception is the coal mining area in West Virginia.

Not only is the Appalachian nonwhite population very small, but it is also decreasing. Between 1950 and 1960 the white population decreased by 2.5 percent as compared to 6.2 percent for the nonwhite population (Table 4). This was counter to the national trend where nonwhites increased at a rate (27.0 percent) considerably above that for whites (17.4 percent). In view of the higher fertility among Appalachian non-whites (a 1960 fertility ratio of 631 compared to 512 for whites) population decline is attributable primarily to out-

TABLE 4

Percentage Change in Population, by Race, for the Southern Appalachian Region and the United States, 1950-1960

Area	Total	White	Nonwhite
Southern Appalachians	−2.8	−2.5	−6.2
United States	18.5	17.4	27.0

SOURCES: Compiled from *U.S. Census of Population, 1960*, and James S. Brown, Basic Population Data for the Southern Appalachians, University of Kentucky Social Research Service, 1958.

migration. It seems probable, therefore, that the out-migration rate for nonwhites exceeded that for whites during the 1950 decade.

A convenient way to summarize age data is to compute the

TABLE 5

Percentage Distribution of the Population by Life Stages for the Southern Appalachian Region and the United States, 1960

Life Stage	Southern Appalachians	United States
Childhood (under 10 years)	21.3	21.8
Youth (10–19 years)	20.0	16.7
Young adults (20–39 years)	24.7	25.7
Middle-aged (40–64 years)	25.5	26.6
Aged (65 years and over)	8.5	9.2

SOURCES: Compiled from *U.S. Census of Population, 1960*, and James S. Brown, Basic Population Data for the Southern Appalachians, University of Kentucky Social Research Service, 1958.

proportion of the total population at various stages in the life cycle. As can be seen in Table 5, the 1960 Southern Appalachian population had a considerably higher proportion of youths but a slightly lower proportion of young-adult, middle-aged, and older persons than the national average. The higher proportion of youths undoubtedly reflects the "baby boom" of the late 1940s. However, the percentage is also affected by fewer persons in the adult categories as a result of heavy out-migration. The young-adult group is, of course, of prime importance in fertility research, since birth rates are highest among those at this stage in life.

Although the 1960 Appalachian and United States age structures bear some resemblance, the changes during the decade 1950-1960 are different (Table 6). An important national

TABLE 6

Percentage Change in Population by Life Stages for the Southern Appalachian Region and the United States, 1950–1960

Life Stage	Southern Appalachians	United States
Childhood (under 10 years)	–10.6	32.2
Youth (10–19 years)	3.2	37.3
Young adults (20–39 years)	–18.7	–1.3
Middle-aged (40-64 years)	12.0	16.3
Aged (65 years and over)	13.0	34.7

SOURCES: Compiled from *U.S. Census of Population, 1960,* and James S. Brown, Basic Population Data for the Southern Appalachians, University of Kentucky Social Research Service, 1958.

trend was an increase of about one-third in the number of children and youths, but the number of Appalachian youths stayed about the same, while the number of younger children actually decreased by more than 10 percent. Closely related to this trend is the decrease by nearly one-fourth in the number of young adults in the region. The influence of migration in alteration of the age structure is apparent.

Compared to the nation, the older aged population of the Southern Appalachians did not increase very rapidly between 1950 and 1960. Nevertheless, the 13 and 12 percent increases in the number of older and middle-aged adults, respectively, were by far greater than for any other age group.

SOCIAL CHARACTERISTICS

In addition to the age and racial composition several social characteristics of the population can influence human behavior. Two of the more important are marital status and education. In the Southern Appalachians and in the nation two out of three people aged fourteen and over were married (Table 7). In general the 1950–1960 data show an increase in the proportion of the population reported as married, especially for men. One notable difference between regional and national trends was that the proportion of married women in Appalachia declined from 66.3 percent in 1950 to 64.5 percent in 1960, while the national proportion increased slightly from 65.8 to 65.9 percent.

TABLE 7

Percentage Distribution by Marital Status of the Population 14 Years Old and Over, by Sex, for the Southern Appalachian Region and the United States, 1950 and 1960

Marital Status	SOUTHERN APPALACHIANS				UNITED STATES			
	Males		Females		Males		Females	
	1960	1950	1960	1950	1960	1950	1960	1950
Single	26.4	27.8	20.3	21.5	25.1	26.4	19.1	20.0
Married	68.6	67.3	65.5	66.3	69.1	67.5	65.9	65.8
Widowed or Divorced	5.0	4.9	14.2	12.2	5.8	6.1	15.0	14.2

SOURCES: Compiled from *U.S. Census of Population, 1960,* and James S. Brown, Basic Population Data for the Southern Appalachians, University of Kentucky Social Research Service, 1958.

Single status was reported by about one-fourth of the males and one-fifth of the females in Appalachia. The proportion of both single males and single females was above the national levels in 1950 and 1960. However, the overall trend was much the same—a decrease in the proportion of single persons.

The most notable differences were in the widowed or divorced category. As indicated in Table 7 the proportion of widowed females was more than two-and-one-half times that for males. In comparison to the nation Appalachia had a lower proportion of widowed or divorced males and females in both 1950 and 1960.

Between 1950 and 1960 the proportion of widowed or divorced males remained about the same, but the proportion of females in this category increased, particularly in the Appalachians (from 12.2 percent to 14.2 percent). Increases in the length of life for both sexes has meant that marriages last longer before they are broken by death. However, women have longer life expectancies than men, and this, combined with the fact that women usually marry men older than themselves, results in a higher proportion of widowed women and a decrease in the proportion of women married.

The general education level of Appalachia is known to be below the national level. As measured by median years of school completed for the population aged twenty-five and over, the 1960 level of 8.6 years completed was below the national norm by two years. This also was slightly lower than the 8.7 level for Kentucky, which had the most poorly

TABLE 8

Percentage Distribution of Years of School Completed by Persons Aged 25 Years and Over for the Southern Appalachian Region and the United States, 1960

Years of School Completed		Southern Appalachian	United States
No years completed		2.7	2.3
Elementary:	1–4 years	12.8	6.1
	5–7 years	24.6	13.9
	8 years	17.1	17.5
High School:	1–3 years	15.4	19.2
	4 years	16.3	24.6
College:	1–3 years	6.2	8.8
	4 or more	4.9	7.7

SOURCES: Compiled from *U.S. Census of Population, 1960,* and James S. Brown, Basic Population Data for the Southern Appalachians, University of Kentucky Social Research Service, 1958.

educated white population in the nation.[6] A factor contributing to the low level of education of the Appalachian adult population is out-migration, which tends to be selective of younger, better educated, adults.

Table 8 shows that the differences between Appalachia and the nation are particularly marked in the high and low educational categories. More than 15 percent, or 460,500, of Appalachia's population aged twenty-five and over in 1960 were functionally illiterate, having completed four years of school or less. The national figure, which included data on Appalachia, was 8.4 percent. At the other extreme 27 percent of Appalachia's adult population had completed at least four years of high school, compared to 41 percent of the national population, and one Appalachian adult in twenty had finished college, compared to one in thirteen for the nation.

TABLE 9

Median Years of School Completed by Persons Aged 25 Years and Over for the Southern Appalachian Region and the United States, 1950 and 1960

Area	1960	1950
Southern Appalachians	8.6	8.0
United States	10.6	9.3

SOURCES: Compiled from *U.S. Census of Population, 1960,* and James S. Brown, Basic Population Data for the Southern Appalachians, University of Kentucky Social Research Service, 1958.

Although the median education level in Appalachia increased from 8.0 to 8.6 between 1950 and 1960, the rate of increase lagged behind the national level, which rose from 9.3 to 10.6 years (Table 9). Thus, Appalachia's 1960 level of educational attainment represented a relative regression from 1950. The low educational level and the trend toward a more unfavorable position in comparison to the nation has serious social and economic implications for the region's

[6] Thomas R. Ford, *Health and Demography in Kentucky* (Lexington: University of Kentucky Press, 1964), 57-58.

FIGURE 2

Population Growth of the Southern Appalachian Region and the United States, 1900-1960

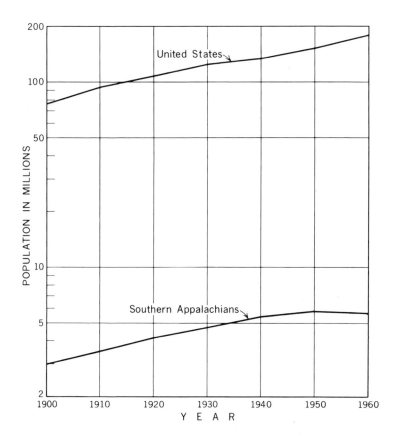

SOURCE: Compiled from *U.S. Census of Population, 1960,* and James S. Brown, Basic Population Data for the Southern Appalachians, University of Kentucky Social Research Service, 1958.

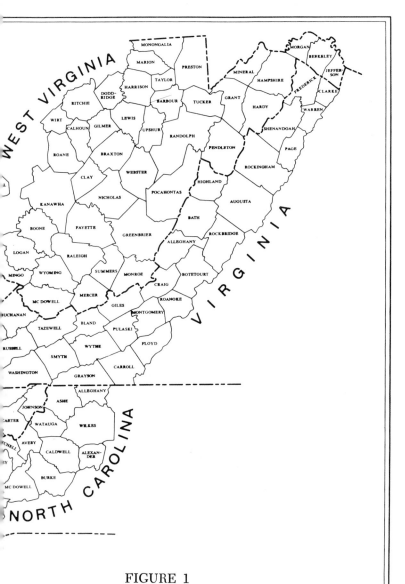

FIGURE 1

The Region as Defined in 1960

THE SOUTHERN APPALACHIANS

SCALE
10   0   10   20   30   40   50 MILES

N

KENTUCKY

LEWIS · GREENUP · CAB
CARTER · BOYD
ROWAN · ELLIOTT · LAWRENCE · WAYNE
MENIFEE · MORGAN · JOHNSON · MARTIN
POWELL · WOLFE · MAGOFFIN
ESTILL · LEE · BREATHITT · FLOYD · PIKE
JACKSON · OWSLEY · PERRY · KNOTT
CLAY · LESLIE · LETCHER · DICKENS
LAUREL · WISE
KNOX · HARLAN
WHITLEY · BELL · LEE · SCOTT
MC CREARY

TENNESSEE

HANCOCK · SULLIV
CLAIBORNE · HAWKINS
FENTRESS · SCOTT · CAMPBELL · GRAINGER · WASHING TON
UNION · HAMBLEN · GREENE
MORGAN · ANDERSON · KNOX · JEFFERSON · UNION
CUMBERLAND · COCKE · MADISON · YA
ROANE · SEVIER
VAN BUREN · LOUDON · BLOUNT
RHEA · SWAIN · HAYWOOD · BUNCOMBE
BLEDSOE · MONROE · GRAHAM · JACKSON · HENDERSO
GRUNDY · SEQUATCHIE · MEIGS · MC MINN · TRANSYL-VANIA
HAMILTON · MACON
MARION · Chattanooga · BRADLEY · POLK · CHEROKEE · CLAY

ALABAMA

DADE · ATOO · CLAY · FANNIN · TOWNS · RABUN
JACKSON · WHIT-FIELD · MURRAY · UNION
WALKER · GILMER · HABER-SHAM
CHATTOOGA · WHITE
MARSHALL · DE KALB · GORDON · PICKENS · LUMPKIN
CULLMAN · FLOYD · BARTOW · DAWSON
BLOUNT · POLK

GEORGIA

W. VA · KY · VA · TENN · NC · SC · ALA · GA

FIGURE 3

Distribution of Families by Amount of 1959 Income, by Percentage, for the Southern Appalachian Region and the United States

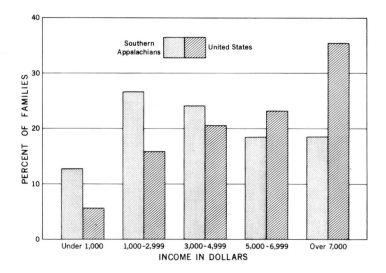

SOURCE: Compiled from *U.S. Census of Population, 1960,* and James S. Brown, Basic Population Data for the Southern Appalachians, University of Kentucky Social Research Service, 1958.

problems. Educational attainment is one of the most important indicators of human resource potential and a critical component in the development process. In this study the educational levels and trends constitute important parts of the social milieu bearing upon Appalachian fertility.

ECONOMIC CHARACTERISTICS

Without doubt economic characteristics are the most widely discussed aspects of the population of Appalachia. This is particularly true about level of income, which has become the prime determining factor in government antipoverty programs. In view of the important linkage between economic characteristics and the fertility of a population, economic information is essential to an understanding of fertility.

Many changes have taken place in the structure of the Appalachian economy in the past few years. Some have been well publicized, such as the technological changes that have displaced workers in the coal mines. But there have been other changes, some of which are reflected in shifts in the labor force and the industrial and occupational structure of

TABLE 10

Labor Force Characteristics, by Sex, for the Southern Appalachian Region and the United States, 1950 and 1960

Area and Sex	Percent of Total Population 14 and Over in Labor Force		Percent Unemployed	
	1960	1950	1960	1950
SOUTHERN APPALACHIANS				
Males	69.0	75.0	7.3	4.2
Females	25.0	20.6	5.7	4.4
UNITED STATES				
Males	77.4	78.8	5.0	4.9
Females	34.5	28.9	5.4	4.6

SOURCES: Compiled from *U.S. Census of Population, 1960,* and James S. Brown, Basic Population Data for the Southern Appalachians, University of Kentucky Social Research Service, 1958.

the area. One of the more notable features of the makeup of the labor force has been the significant shift in the sex composition (Table 10). During the 1950s the male members of the labor force—which consists of unemployed persons who are seeking employment as well as those who are employed—decreased by nearly 200,000. In 1960 some 69 percent of the total Appalachian male population aged fourteen and over was in the labor force, compared to more than 77 percent for the nation. While the male labor force decreased, the female labor force increased by 130,000 from 20.6 percent of the total female population aged fourteen and over in 1950 to 25.0 percent in 1960. However, this figure was still below the 34.5 percent of females in the labor force of the United States. In both decades the unemployment rate for both Appalachian males and females was higher than comparable rates for the nation, .and the difference was greater in 1960 than in 1950.

Although these changes in the labor force composition primarily reflect shifts in the economic structure, the effects are not restricted to the economy. They contain significant implications for the traditional sex roles in Appalachian society. Forced into idleness by changes in the economic structure, many mountain men can no longer support their wives and families. As the husband's role has altered, an increasing number of mountain women have abandoned traditional norms and have sought employment. This situation leads to a reversal in the roles of the sexes and to changes in the social organization of the family. If past research is an accurate guide, such changes frequently influence fertility and family size.

In addition to the changing composition of the labor force there have been equally dramatic transformations in the industrial and occupational structure of Appalachia. One of the most outdated stereotypes is the image of Appalachian economy as dominated by subsistence agriculture and mining. In 1960 less than three male workers in ten were employed in agriculture, forestry, fisheries, mining, and construction combined (Table 11). By comparison, approximately an equal number of male workers were employed in manufacturing; and with the increased participation of women in the labor

TABLE 11

Employed Persons in the Southern Appalachian Region and
the United States by Major Industry Group with Percentage
Distribution, by Sex, 1960

Industry Group	SOUTHERN APPALACHIANS Male	Female	UNITED STATES Male	Female
Agriculture, forestry and fisheries	11.6	2.0	9.0	2.0
Construction and mining	17.6	0.8	9.9	0.9
Manufacturing	28.6	25.2	30.2	20.8
Transportation, communications and public utilities	8.5	2.9	8.5	3.6
Wholesale and retail trade	15.2	20.2	17.0	20.7
Finance, insurance and real estate	1.8	3.0	3.4	5.8
Business repair services	2.3	0.8	2.9	1.6
Personal services	2.3	14.3	2.5	13.1
Entertainment and recreation services	0.6	0.5	0.8	0.7
Professional and related services	5.9	22.8	6.9	21.5
Public administration	3.1	3.1	5.3	4.3
Industry not reported	2.5	4.4	3.6	4.8

SOURCE: Compiled from *U.S. Census of Population, 1960.*

force the total employment in manufacturing industries in
1960 surpassed that in agriculture, mining, and related industries by more than 100,000.

The shift toward an industrial base can be demonstrated
by analyzing decade changes in employment by industry
(Table 12). Between 1950 and 1960 employment in manufacturing increased by nearly 20 percent for males and 36
percent for females. Comparable increases for the nation
were 19 and 20 percent, respectively. At the same time employment in Appalachia of males in agriculture, forestry,
and fisheries declined by more than 55 percent, and mining
and construction employment by 35 percent. Industries showing notable employment gains in Appalachia were the same

TABLE 12

Percentage Change in the Industrial Composition of Employed Persons, by Sex, for the Southern Appalachian Region and the United States, 1950–1960

Industry Group	SOUTHERN APPALACHIANS		UNITED STATES	
	Male	Female	Male	Female
Agriculture, forestry and fisheries	–55.8	–34.2	–38.9	–29.5
Construction and mining	–35.0	– 5.6	0.4	51.7
Manufacturing	19.6	.35.8	18.9	20.4
Transportation, communications and public utilities	– 9.2	14.9	– 1.7	10.3
Wholesale and retail trade	7.4	17.2	6.5	23.5
Finance, insurance and real estate	36.1	68.2	28.7	57.3
Business repair services	–11.7	78.1	10.8	111.5
Personal services	– 6.6	13.0	– 7.0	20.6
Entertainment and recreation services	–26.1	4.5	– 5.8	24.1
Professional and related services	36.2	55.5	48.0	63.6
Public administration	10.8	19.2	23.3	38.8

SOURCE: Compiled from *U.S. Census of Population, 1950 and 1960.*

ones showing increases throughout the nation—finance, professional, and public administration fields.

These changes have brought the industrial composition of the Appalachian labor force much closer to the composition of the national labor force. For example, nearly 29 percent of the region's employed males in 1960 were engaged in manufacturing, compared to 30 percent for the nation. Twelve percent were employed in agriculture, forestry, and fisheries, compared to 9 percent for the entire United States (Table 11). The greatest discrepancy was in mining and construction, which employs about 18 percent of the region's male labor force but only about 10 percent of the nation's. In general, smaller proportions of Appalachian men than all men in the nation were employed in professional, public administration, and commercial service industries.

The largest increase in female employment was not in manufacturing but in professional and related services in which employment increased by 42,000, or 55 percent, during the 1950s. This is compared to an increase of 35,000, or 36 percent, in manufacturing. In fact, a greater proportion of women in Appalachia than in the nation were employed in these two industrial categories in 1960.

The economic transformation of Appalachia so evident in the industrial composition is also reflected in the occupational structure. In 1960, one employed Appalachian male in four had a white-collar occupation, compared with one in three for the nation (Table 13). However, between 1950 and 1960 the proportion of white-collar male workers in Appalachia increased at a greater rate than for the nation—from 20.4 to 26.7 percent, compared to 30.8 to 34.8 percent for the nation. Professional occupations showed the greatest proportional gain.

By far the largest occupational groups in the Southern Appalachians in 1960 were the operators and kindred workers with 27.3 percent, and craftsmen, foremen, and kindred workers with 19.1 percent. Although the proportion classified as operators declined slightly during the 1950–1960 decade, the Appalachian figure of 27.3 percent was well above the national level of 19.9 percent. For the same period craftsmen, foremen, and kindred workers had the greatest proportional increase of any occupational group for employed males—from 15.6 percent in 1950 to 19.1 percent in 1960.

As would be expected, farmers and farm managers constituted a larger proportion of Appalachia's 1960 male labor force than of the nation's, although the differences were not great—7.5 percent compared to 5.5 percent, and the proportion was only one-half what it was in 1950 for both the region and the nation. There was also a marked decline in the proportion of farm laborers in both areas. Clearly in Appalachia, as in the nation, the economy has shifted from a reliance upon agriculture and mining to a reliance upon manufacturing and commerce. As a basic factor in social mobility, this change

TABLE 13

Percentage Distribution of Occupational Groups of Employed Males in the Southern Appalachian Region and the United States, 1960 and 1950

Occupational Group	SOUTHERN APPALACHIANS 1960	1950	UNITED STATES 1960	1950
Professional, technical, and kindred workers	7.3	4.7	10.3	7.3
Farmers and farm managers	7.5	15.2	5.5	10.4
Managers, officials, and proprietors, except farm	8.7	7.3	10.7	10.7
Clerical and kindred workers	5.0	3.9	6.9	6.5
Sales workers	5.7	4.5	6.9	6.3
Craftsmen, foremen, and kindred workers	19.1	15.6	19.5	18.6
Operatives and kindred workers	27.3	28.9	19.9	20.1
Private household workers	0.2	—	0.1	. 0.2
Service workers, except private household	4.4	3.7	6.0	5.8
Farm laborers and foremen	3.3	7.1	2.8	4.9
Laborers, except farm and mine	7.7	7.7	6.9	8.1
Occupation not reported	3.8	1.4	4.6	1.1

SOURCES: Compiled from *U.S. Census of Population, 1960*, and James S. Brown, Basic Population Data for the Southern Appalachians, University of Kentucky Social Research Service, 1958.

complements the rural-to-urban shift in geographic mobility, and both trends are important in understanding the changes in fertility.

Although the industrial and occupational composition of the Appalachian labor force definitely has been altered, the present economic structure provides fulltime employment for a substantially smaller proportion of the potential labor force than is true for the national economy. In addition, the wage scale is generally lower, and thus the overall family income also is lower. The median income of Southern Appalachian families in 1959 was $3,882, or about 60 percent of the national median of $5,657 (Table 14). Median income, though a con-

TABLE 14

Median Income for Families in the Southern Appalachian Region and the United States, 1959 and 1949

Area	1959	1949
Southern Appalachians	$3,882	$2,112
United States	$5,657	$3,083
Appalachian median as percentage of U.S.	68.6	68.5

SOURCES: Compiled from *U.S. Census of Population, 1960*, and James S. Brown, Basic Population Data for the Southern Appalachians, University of Kentucky Social Research Service, 1958.

venient summary statistic, does not indicate the range of family incomes, however. Percentage distributions of the 1959 income level of Appalachian and United States families are presented graphically in Figure 3 (p. 22).

One Appalachian family in eight had an income of less than one thousand dollars, compared to only one family in twenty for the nation. Based on the popular poverty designation of an income below three thousand dollars a year, nearly 40 percent of the Appalachian families were at the poverty level. On the other extreme about 18 percent of the families in Appalachia and 35 percent in the nation reported an income of seven thousand dollars or more.

Despite the substandard level, family income in Appalachia increased substantially during the 1950 decade. Unfortunately, the figures for the 1950 and 1960 periods are not completely comparable. In the 1950 census the income of the head of household was assumed to be the total income for the family if no other members reported an income. In 1960 other family members who failed to report an income were assigned the reported income of persons with similar demographic characteristics. The exact effect of this on comparability is unknown, but if it is assumed that the effect was roughly the same for the Appalachians and the nation, it is possible to make general comparisons.

Since 1949 the median income for Appalachian families increased by about $1,700, while the comparable increase for the nation was $2,574. In spite of the considerable difference in the increase of incomes in dollars, the percentage of increase for the two regions was about the same at 84 percent. Not all the increment represented a gain in real purchasing power, however, since the national consumer-price index rose from 101.8 to 124.6 between 1949 and 1959.[7] If it is assumed that the rise in the cost of living in Appalachia was the same as the rise throughout the nation, the "real" increase in family income was about 50 percent from both areas.

From this brief analysis one can obtain a general picture of the demographic factors that form the backdrop for an analysis of Appalachian fertility. On many of the social and economic indicators the region compares poorly with the nation. Nevertheless, it is slowly becoming more integrated into the national population.

[7] U.S. Bureau of the Census, *U.S. Census of Population: 1960*, PC(1)-IC, p. xxxix.

2. Fertility Patterns

"The fertile mountains" is a phrase that accurately reflects the image many Americans have of the Appalachians. Not that the land is fertile; in fact, the opposite would be more appropriate. The phrase refers rather to the reproductive prowess of the residents, a prowess attested to by many writers.

A graphic picture of high fertility in the Appalachians appeared in a popular weekly magazine in 1949.[1] Taking Leslie County, Kentucky, as an example, the author found that the area had a chronic baby boom, which he characterized as a source to replenish the nation's population. Indeed, the rate of population increase was comparable to that of India or China. The author found that families of ten and twelve children were common; but the average was about six or seven.[2] Marriage for most women came at age sixteen or seventeen, although fifteen was not an uncommon age for brides. And although birth control information was available and contraceptives relatively inexpensive, very few people expressed an interest in using them. Thus, it comes as little surprise to discover that the 1950 birth rate of Leslie County was much the same as it was in the frontier days of 1830.

The traditionally high fertility patterns of the Appalachians are nowhere more striking than when compared to national trends. Historically, fertility declined in most sections of the nation with the passing of the frontier.[3] However, the Southeast, which includes the Southern Appalachian Region, remained an area of outstanding high fertility. Even during the Depression of the 1930s, when birth rates for most areas of the nation were quite low, this section deviated notably.

During the Depression President Franklin D. Roosevelt asked his science committee to prepare a report on the major problems of human resources. This report, which furnished basic information for policy decisions, concerned the entire country but devoted considerable attention to Appalachia. Even then the committee noted a serious overpopulation of the area in relation to its economic opportunities. A primary reason was clear. "The highest fertility in the United States is found among the women of the Southern Appalachians. If there were no emigration, the population of counties of southern West Virginia, southwestern Virginia, western North Carolina, eastern Kentucky, and eastern Tennessee would double within one generation."[4] The similarity between the committee's diagnoses of Appalachia and the findings of more recent government investigations of Appalachian counties is striking.

Although many others have commented on high fertility patterns in the Southern Appalachians,[5] perhaps the most thorough investigation was made by Gilbert W. Beebe in the latter 1930s.[6] His basic point of departure was that poverty and high fertility are interrelated and that attempts to lower fertility would in some degree contribute to an improvement in the level of living or at least arrest its further deterioration.

He proposed to investigate the possibility that rural women of high fertility could be encouraged to practice birth control. An intensive study of 1,300 families in Logan County, West Virginia, was initiated. With the aid of medical and public health officials birth control information and contraceptives were made available to the sample population. Careful analysis of the two-year project indicated that while the participants had a general desire to limit family size, they showed

[1] T. S. Hyland, "The Fruitful Mountaineer," *Life*, XXVII (Dec. 26, 1949), 60-67.

[2] *Ibid.*, 60.

[3] Rupert B. Vance, *All These People* (Chapel Hill: University of North Carolina Press, 1945), 62-108.

[4] National Resources Committee, *The Problems of a Changing Population* (Washington, 1938), 52, 122.

[5] See, for instance, L. C. Gray, *Economic and Social Problems of the Southern Appalachians*, U.S. Dept. of Agriculture Miscellaneous Publication 205 (Washington, 1935), 5; Carle C. Zimmerman and Richard F. DuWors, *Graphic Regional Sociology* (Cambridge, Mass.: The Phillips Book Store, 1952), 45, 53; T. Lynn Smith, *Fundamentals of Population Study* (New York: J. B. Lippincott, 1960), 309-11; Vance, *All These People*, 62-108; and John C. Belcher, "Population Growth and Characteristics," *SAR*, 43-51.

[6] Gilbert W. Beebe, *Conception and Fertility in the Southern Appalachians* (Baltimore: Williams and Wilkins, 1942).

such a low acceptance of birth control methods that the programs could not be expected to have a long-term effect on fertility.

Clearly, Beebe chose the Southern Appalachians as a laboratory for his research because it was the most obvious example of the familiar interlaced pattern of want, meager resources, and high fertility. He found that the reproduction rate in the area was comparable to that of the more urban seaboard center of the early 1800s, when fertility had just begun to decline. Also, he found the area was largely bypassed by the patterns of family limitation that have traveled in the wake of industrialization and urbanization.

More than two decades have passed since Beebe's investigation, and with other societal changes it is questionable whether the image of the "fertile mountains" accurately reflects the current pattern in the Southern Appalachians. An examination of the fertility rates in the 190 counties included in the region and the changes in these rates during the three decades from 1930 to 1960 will help to answer this question.

Several possible measures of fertility can be used in an analysis. Perhaps the most common indicator of fertility is the crude birth rate.[7] However, as the name indicates, it is a gross measure of fertility and is, for instance, insensitive to alterations in the age and sex structure of the population. The fertility ratio, or child-woman ratio as it is also called, has an advantage over the crude birth rate, because the number of women in the reproductive age group rather than the total population is used as the denominator. The general fertility rate combines some desirable features of the crude birth rate and the fertility ratio, but it is also subject to many of the same limitations. Of particular concern is the timespan of the birth data on which the measure is based. The five-year pe-

---

[7] The crude birth rate is the annual number of births per 1,000 in the total population. The fertility ratio is the number of children in the age group of four and below per 1,000 women in the reproductive span (usually women aged fifteen to forty-four). The general fertility rate has elements of both the crude birth rate and the fertility ratio—births per year (as does the crude birth rate) and women in the childbearing age groups (as does the fertility ratio). The general fertility rate is defined as the annual number of births per 1,000 women in the reproductive age groups.

riod used to compute the fertility ratio can obscure relatively short-term features, but the one-year period used as a basis for the crude birth rate is susceptible to yearly variations, especially in many Appalachian counties where birth registration is not entirely complete. Because of these limitations a three-year average of registered births was computed.

To obtain a maximum of information about the Southern Appalachian Region fertility patterns all three measures were computed—the crude birth rate, the fertility ratio, and the general fertility rate. By using all three, one can study several dimensions of fertility, since each taps a different aspect. In subsequent chapters when it is necessary to use only a single measure, however, the general fertility rate will be used.

The major sources of data were census and vital statistics reports.[8] The decision to restrict the analysis to the years 1930, 1940, 1950, and 1960 was dictated primarily by the unavailability and poor quality of data prior to 1930.

In addition, the data were adjusted for anticipated errors. Possible errors arising from yearly variations in the number of registered births were offset by computing an average figure that included registered births for the years immediately before and after a census year. Mean crude birth rates were computed for the years 1929–1931, 1939–1941, 1949–1951, and 1959–1960, using the decennial census population as the denominator in each case.[9] The same birth data were used in computing the general fertility rates. A further adjustment corrected for the underregistration of births. Births for both the 1929–1931 and the 1939–1941 periods were adjusted for underregistration by the use of the 1940 county registration completeness factors.[10] Adjustment for 1959–1960 underregistration was made by using the midpoint between 1950 registration completeness and 100 percent. No adjustments were made for the underenumeration of children in computing

---

[8] For a complete list of sources of the data see Appendix B.

[9] Final registered birth data for 1961 were not available for all counties at the time these rates were calculated.

[10] National Office of Vital Statistics, *Vital Statistics—Special Reports,* XVII (18) (April 1953), Table 1; and XXXIX (4), part 2 (Jan. 1955), Table 1.

fertility ratios; thus, the ratios may be underestimated, especially in the earlier years.

The plan to compare population groups in differing locations and at differing times raises the question of whether or not valid analyses can be obtained with the crude measures of fertility previously mentioned. Researchers in demography are constantly warning of the danger in making comparative analyses of two or more population groups, or even of the same population at differing time periods, without controlling for differences in the age distribution.

As a control for these variations in age structure, the female population in each of the region's 190 counties for the years 1930, 1940, 1950, and 1960 was indirectly standardized by using the United States age-specific general fertility rates for 1950.[11] This additional measure of fertility makes possible a comparison of county rates, with the age composition statistically controlled, for a given decade and for the entire 1930–1960 period.

Fertility rates at the beginning of each decade are shown in Table 15. Because of computational differences in the various measures, rates given for the same years actually reflect fertility for different years. The fertility ratio for 1950, for example, includes children born in the peak birth year of 1947, but these are not represented in the crude birth rate or the general fertility rate, which for 1950 are based on average annual births for 1949, 1950, and 1951. Nevertheless, Southern Appalachian fertility rates were 50 to 60 percent higher than comparable national rates for the white population in 1930 but were about equal to or slightly lower than national rates on all measures in 1960.

Although the long-term trends are the same on each measure for the 1930–1960 period, the various measures reveal different short-term trends. The crude birth rate, which in 1930 stood at 30.1, was virtually unchanged in 1940. By 1950

[11] For discussions of standardization see Abram J. Jaffe, *Handbook of Statistical Methods for Demographers* (Washington: U.S. Bureau of the Census, 1960), 43-52; George W. Barclay, *Techniques of Population Analysis* (New York: John Wiley, 1958), 161-66; and Mortimer Spiegelman, *Introduction to Demography* (Chicago: The Society of Actuaries, 1955), 66-69.

TABLE 15

Measures of Fertility for the White Population of the Southern Appalachian Region: 1930, 1940, 1950, and 1960

Fertility Measure	Appalachian Rate				As Percentage of U.S. Rate			
	1930	1940	1950	1960	1930	1940	1950	1960
Crude birth rate[a]	30.1	30.2	28.0	23.0	146.1	162.4	121.7	100.9
Fertility ratio	585.0	480.6	549.6	511.5	150.0	148.7	117.7	93.7
General fertility rate[a]	135.7	127.4	124.8	111.0	157.8	163.3	122.0	97.5
Standardized general fertility rate[b]	129.5	122.0	122.9	117.8	152.9	151.4	120.1	99.1

[a] Based on average annual births in the Southern Appalachian Region for periods 1929–1931, 1939–1941, 1949–1951, and 1959–1960, adjusted for underregistration.

[b] Indirectly standardized using five-year age-specific birth rates for U.S. native white women, 1950.

it was only slightly lower at 28.0; however, the 1960 rate was 23.0, a considerable decline from the 1950 figure. According to Belcher,[12] the crude birth rate for the total population of the region was higher throughout most of the last half of the 1940–1950 decade than it was in 1940 and declined below the national crude birth rate as early as 1952. Belcher did not make adjustments for underregistration, however, so the drop to the national level probably occurred later than his figures indicate.

Unlike the crude birth rate, the fertility ratio declined sharply from 585 in 1930 to 481 in 1940. This decline probably reflects a lower average birth rate during the years 1935 through 1938 than for 1939 through 1941, which would be in keeping with the national trend for that period. The ratio increased sharply to 550 in 1950 after the postwar baby boom, but the 1960 rate of 512 was about 7 percent lower than in 1950. The fertility ratio for the nation's white population rose by about 17 percent between 1950 and 1960, so it is a plausible hypothesis that the regional decline came about through selective migration of young families.

The unstandardized general fertility rate in the region declined in each successive decade from the 1930 rate of 135.7 to the 1960 level of 111.0, a drop of about 18 percent. Standardization reduces this difference between the extremes of the thirty-year period by one-half. The 1950 standardized general fertility rate of 122.9 was slightly higher than the 1960 rate of 117.8. It is evident, therefore, that the decline in fertility between 1950 and 1960 was influenced by factors other than changes in the age composition of the female population, although this did have an appreciable effect. The unstandardized general fertility rate declined 11 percent between 1950 and 1960, but with standardization the decline was slightly more than 4 percent.

The decline in fertility was not uniform for all Appalachian counties. In fact, the variation between county fertility rates is a salient feature of the data. This variability is evident from Figures 4 and 5, which show counties grouped on the basis of fertility rates for 1930 and 1960.

[12] Belcher, "Population Growth," *SAR*, 50.

In 1930 nearly one-third of the 190 counties had a general fertility rate of 160 or more and more than one-half of the counties had a rate of 140 or more. At this time the general fertility rate for the nation was 86. No more than 5 percent of all the counties in Appalachia had a rate of less than 100 births per 1,000 women in the 15 through 44 age group.

Not only the variation in county fertility rates but also the level of fertility in the Southern Appalachian Region had changed considerably by 1960. In 1930 about 50 percent of the counties had a rate of 140 or more, but in 1960 nearly 67 percent of the counties had a rate of less than 120. Only about 3 percent of Appalachia's counties had 1960 general fertility rates of 160 or more. For both time periods the area with the highest fertility rate was eastern Kentucky. The decade-to-decade changes in fertility will be considered in more detail in the next section.

One way to summarize changes in county fertility rates is to note the decade in which the rates reached the national average. In addition to summarizing fertility trends the tracing of the ecology of fertility change may suggest possible correlates of the decline. If, as hypothesized, migration and attitudes are important factors, one would expect this to be reflected in the ecological patterns.

The demographic and attitudinal variables theoretically would be expected to influence declining fertility in different ways. If migration were a significant factor, lowest fertility rates would be expected in the rural counties where out-migration is the heaviest. On the other hand, if changing cultural factors were of major importance, lowest fertility rates would initially be found in metropolitan counties with the decline later spreading to peripheral counties and the highest rates persisting in the most isolated rural counties. This second line of reasoning is supported not only by general knowledge of fertility patterns but also by Belcher's previous research.[13] The underlying assumption is that metropolitan areas have the greatest cultural change. It would appear that these two lines of investigation are incompatible. However, demographers recognize that both general sociocultural

[13] *Ibid.*, 37-53.

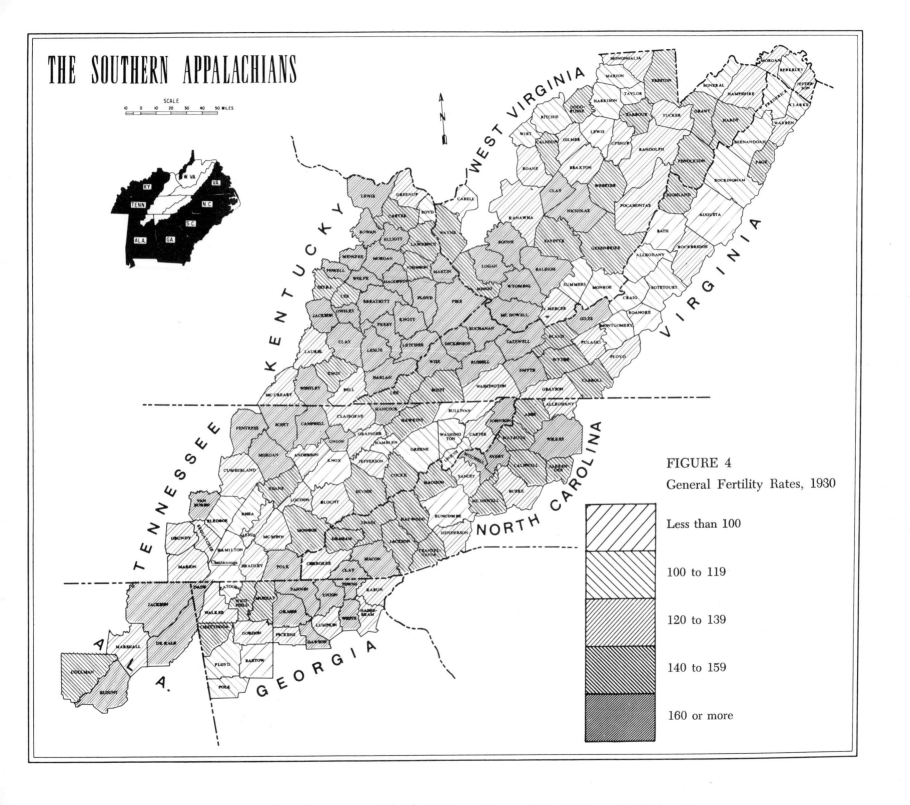

THE SOUTHERN APPALACHIANS

FIGURE 4

General Fertility Rates, 1930

Less than 100

100 to 119

120 to 139

140 to 159

160 or more

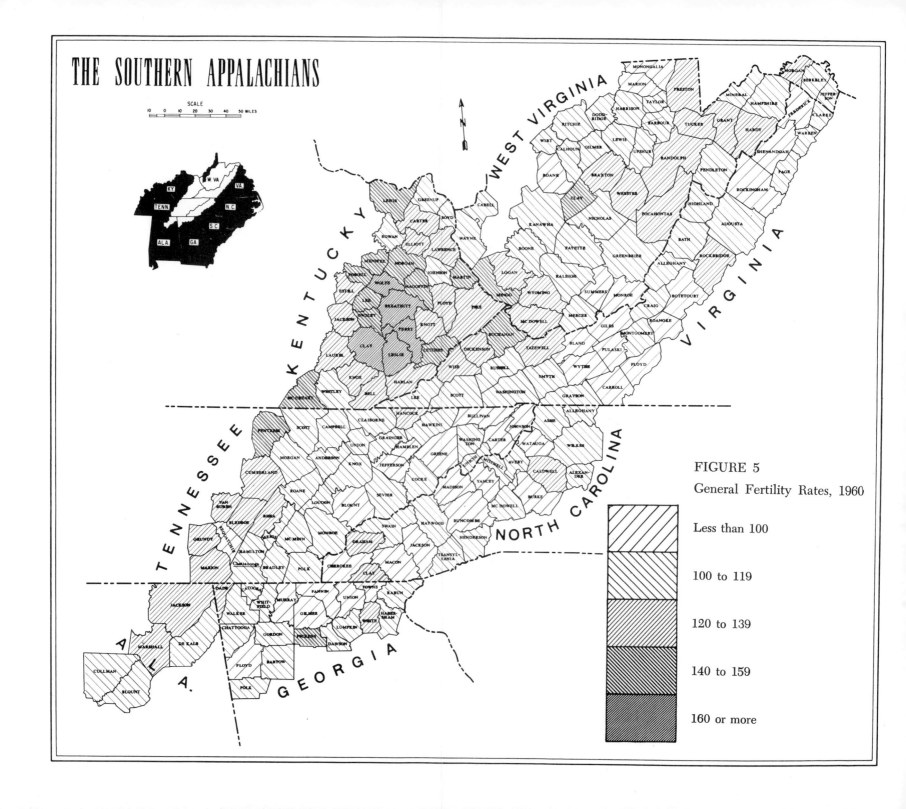

THE SOUTHERN APPALACHIANS

SCALE
10 0 10 20 30 40 50 MILES

FIGURE 5

General Fertility Rates, 1960

Less than 100

100 to 119

120 to 139

140 to 159

160 or more

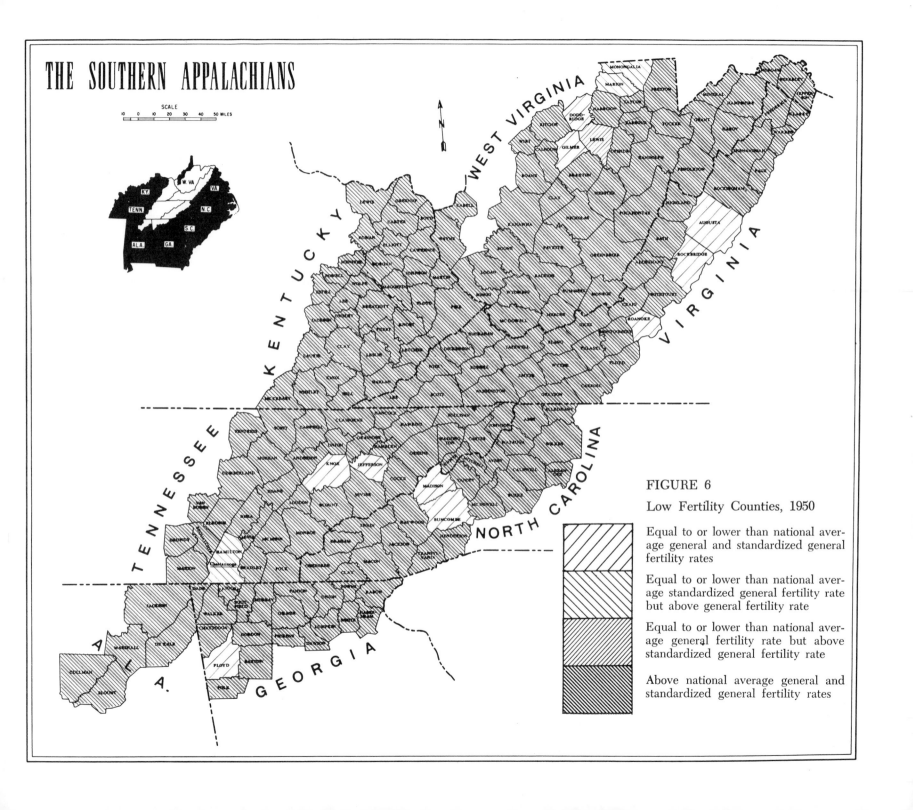

THE SOUTHERN APPALACHIANS

FIGURE 6

Low Fertility Counties, 1950

Equal to or lower than national average general and standardized general fertility rates

Equal to or lower than national average standardized general fertility rate but above general fertility rate

Equal to or lower than national average general fertility rate but above standardized general fertility rate

Above national average general and standardized general fertility rates

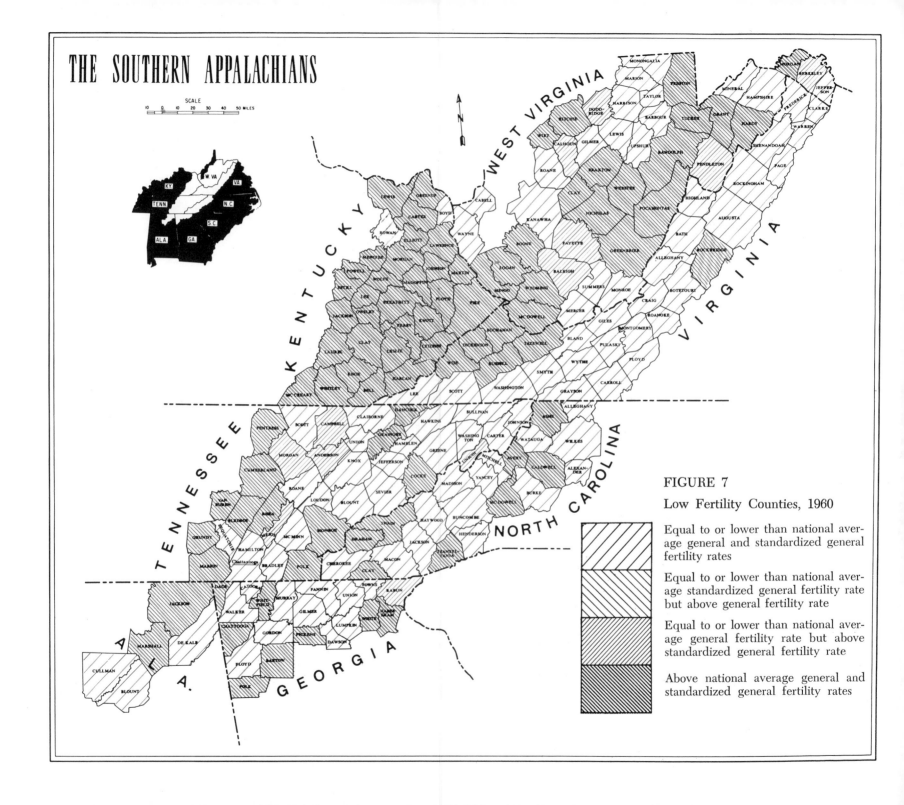

THE SOUTHERN APPALACHIANS

SCALE
10 0 10 20 30 40 50 MILES

FIGURE 7

Low Fertility Counties, 1960

Equal to or lower than national average general and standardized general fertility rates

Equal to or lower than national average standardized general fertility rate but above general fertility rate

Equal to or lower than national average general fertility rate but above standardized general fertility rate

Above national average general and standardized general fertility rates

TABLE 16

Number of Southern Appalachian Counties and Their Percentage of Regional White Population with Unstandardized and Standardized General Fertility Rates Equal to or Lower than National Rates, 1930, 1940, 1950, and 1960

Year	UNSTANDARDIZED		STANDARDIZED[a]	
	Number of Counties	Percentage of Population	Number of Counties	Percentage of Population
1930	3	6.0	3	6.0
1940	—	—	1	0.6
1950	11	8.7	13	13.6
1960	105	66.7	93	59.8

[a] Indirectly standardized using five-year age-specific birth rates for U. S. native white women, 1950.

change and migration can operate to reduce fertility. To trace the geographic distribution of the declining fertility rate in the region the counties were divided according to whether their general fertility rates (a) were equal to or lower than the comparable national rate or (b) exceeded it in each of the years studied. The number of counties with lower or equal rates, both standardized and unstandardized, and the percentage of the regional white population residing in these counties are shown in Table 16.

In 1930, three counties—all in Tennessee—had general fertility rates below the rate for the white population in the United States (86 births per 1,000 women aged 15 through 44 years). These counties represented only 6 percent of the regional white population. Two of them, Hamilton and Knox, contain the cities of Chattanooga and Knoxville, respectively. The third county, Sullivan, contains a portion of the city of Bristol, Tennessee-Virginia, but the extremely low rate recorded for 1930 suggests an error in the registration of births. Births for the independent city of Bristol, Virginia, were combined with those of Washington County, Virginia, and the combined rate was well above the national rate in 1930. Consequently, it seems unlikely that the Tennessee portion of Bristol would have affected the population of Sullivan County in a drastically different manner.

Although the emphasis here is on counties with standardized and unstandardized fertility rates equal to or below the national rate, some counties showed extraordinarily high fertility rates. Highest general fertility rates—about 240 births a year per 1,000 women aged 15-44 years—were recorded in Union County, Tennessee, and Estill and Owsley counties, Kentucky.[14] All three are located in the Cumberland Plateau area on the western rim of the region. In fact, most of the high fertility counties were located in eastern Kentucky, northeastern Tennessee, extreme western Virginia, and southern West Virginia—in general the more rural areas of the region.

In 1940 no Southern Appalachian counties had a general fertility rate lower than the unstandardized national rate of 78, and only one county, Berkeley, West Virginia, had a standardized rate lower than the comparable national figure of 80.6. Berkeley County, which contained less than 1 percent of the region's total 1940 population, is in the eastern Panhandle of West Virginia and is a relatively prosperous farming area in the Shenandoah Valley. Adjacent Morgan and Jefferson counties do not show similar low rates, however, so an error in birth registration for Berkeley County is possible.

As was true in 1930, counties with the highest general fertility rates in 1940 were those located primarily in the plateau areas of Kentucky, Tennessee, and West Virginia, particularly northern Tennessee and eastern Kentucky. However, in most instances the 1940 rates were lower than comparable 1930 figures. Nevertheless, for the region as a whole the general fertility rate declined less rapidly than in the nation (Table 15), and there were fewer counties with rates as low as the national rate in 1940 than there were in 1930.

World War II brought about many changes in the economy and the population of the Southern Appalachian Region. For the metropolitan centers and the mining areas the war and immediate postwar period was one of considerable economic prosperity. It was also a period of accelerated migration. Partly as a consequence of the heavy population loss through migration, the number of births in the region declined sharply

[14] See Appendix A.

after reaching a postwar peak in 1947. Evidence of the effects of migration on fertility can be seen in a comparison of the unstandardized and standardized fertility rates. The unstandardized rate was about 2 percent lower in 1950 than in 1940. On the other hand, the 1950 standardized rate was slightly higher than that of 1940 (Table 15). This means that when the 1940 and 1950 population age structures are statistically controlled (migration is held constant), the 1950 fertility rate is higher than the 1940 rate. However, the unstandardized rate actually was slightly lower than the 1940 rate, indicating that alteration of the age structure, primarily through migration, had occurred.

The slight rise in the standardized general fertility rate and the 2 percent decline in the unstandardized general fertility rate contrasted sharply with the changes for the nation. The United States general fertility rate for whites was 31 percent higher in 1950 than in 1940 on a standardized basis and 27 percent higher on an unstandardized basis. As a consequence of the increase in the national fertility rate and the decline in the regional fertility rate, the number of Southern Appalachian Region counties with rates equal to or lower than the national rate increased.

Counties with standardized and unstandardized general fertility rates equal to or lower than the comparable national rate in 1950 are shown in Figure 6. Eleven counties had unstandardized rates equal to or lower than the national level of 102.3, and ten of these plus two additional counties had equal or lower standardized rates. The eleven counties with unstandardized rates conforming to the national pattern contained about 9 percent of the region's population, and the thirteen counties with low standardized rates contained nearly 14 percent of the regional population (Table 16). Most of the low fertility counties were located in areas of relative economic prosperity. Four of those with lower standardized rates in 1950 are Standard Metropolitan Statistical Area counties containing the central cities of Chattanooga and Knoxville, Tennessee, Asheville, North Carolina, and Roanoke, Virginia. Two other low fertility counties are adjacent to the metropolitan areas of Knoxville and Asheville. Four additional low fertility counties are located in valley areas: Augusta and

Rockingham counties in the Shenandoah Valley of Virginia and Marion and Monongalia counties in the Monongahela Valley of West Virginia.

Again the counties with the highest general fertility rates were those located in the upland areas on the western rim of the region. Magoffin and Leslie counties, Kentucky, were the highest with general fertility rates of more than 200. In general, counties in eastern Kentucky and southern West Virginia continued to be areas of high fertility. Notably, northern Tennessee counties, included as high fertility areas in previous decades, had a considerably lower general fertility rate in 1950 than in 1940.

The great decline in Southern Appalachian fertility came between 1950 and 1960, a period when the general fertility rate for the white population of the nation increased. Consequently, by 1960, 105 Appalachian counties had unstandardized fertility rates equal to or lower than the national rate of 113.9, and 93 counties had standardized rates equal to or lower than the 118.9 national figure. The former counties contained two-thirds of the regional population and the latter about 60 percent (Table 16).

Age standardization reduced by twelve the number of counties with fertility rates below the national level, a fact that supports the hypothesis that selective out-migration was a major factor in the lower fertility. This is because migrants tend to be in the young-adult age groups—the age groups that have the highest fertility rates. When the counties' age structures were standardized, fertility rates were increased in some counties that had experienced sizable migration losses.

The location of the low fertility counties in 1960 is shown in Figure 7. Two features of the map are particularly significant. One is the line of low fertility counties along the eastern edge of the region. This pattern roughly follows the Great Appalachian Valley, which is a series of connected valleys ranging almost the full length of the region. Much of the recent economic development has taken place in the Great Valley.[15]

[15] Charles L. Quittmeyer and Lorin A. Thompson, "The Development of Manufacturing," *SAR*, 123-35.

A second outstanding feature shown in Figure 7 is the location of counties that continue to record fertility rates above the national rate. The largest constellations of high fertility counties are in eastern Kentucky, West Virginia, and on the western edge of the plateau area of Tennessee. Eastern Kentucky counties stand out as the highest fertility areas, particularly Leslie County where the general fertility rate of 235 was extraordinarily high.[16]

Southern Appalachian Region counties with high fertility rates are, in general, the least developed economically. Furthermore, most of these counties had exceedingly high migration losses during the 1950–1960 decade. This would suggest that migration is not as great a factor in reducing regional fertility below the national level as might be expected. Also, the general fertility rate of every Southern Appalachian county included in a Standard Metropolitan Statistical Area in 1960 was below the national rate, and all but one of these either gained population through migration or had relatively small migration losses during the decade.[17] While the causal factors in fertility decline need to be researched further, the extent of the change is quite clear.

[16] See Appendix A.
[17] James S. Brown and George A. Hillery, Jr., "The Great Migration, 1940-1960," *SAR*, 59.

3. Migration and Residence Patterns

The ecological analysis of fertility decline in the preceding chapter suggested the importance of both demographic and sociological factors as influences in the observed changes. The effect of migration on many aspects of the region's social and economic life has been mentioned already. This chapter will consider the consequences of migration on fertility decline.

Migration has become a fact of life for most Southern Appalachian residents desiring a higher level of living. The extent of this outlook on life is suggested by the title of a report by Brown and Hillery "The Great Migration, 1940–1960."[1] There have been numerous researchers who have discussed Appalachian migration.[2] Although these studies have often adopted different approaches to the issue, the major theme has been repetitive—the movement of people from the region.

In the ten-year period between 1950 and 1960 the region had an estimated net loss of 1,108,134 people by migration.[3] This number was equal to almost one-fifth of the area's total 1950 population. For the 1940 to 1950 decade, the estimated net migration loss was somewhat less—705,849. Thus for the two decades the region's estimated net migration loss exceeded the staggering total of 1,800,000 persons.

The exodus trend also is documented by county migration data. Between 1940 and 1950 only fourteen of the 190 Southern Appalachian counties recorded a net migration gain in population. For the 1950 to 1960 decade the number declined to ten counties.[4] This confirms the evidence of increased outmigration and also suggests that most of the region's counties that did gain population can attribute the rise to natural increase rather than to in-migration.

There were, of course, differences in migration for various parts of the region. All three major physiographic divisions had net migration losses, but the Cumberland and Allegheny plateaus experienced by far the greatest losses for both the 1940–1950 and the 1950–1960 decades—minus 18.3 percent and minus 28.3 percent respectively.[5] Losses were particularly heavy in the eastern Kentucky counties. Leslie County, for instance, recorded a 1950–1960 net migration loss of 60.4 percent.[6] The Great Valley, on the other hand, lost less than 10 percent of its population by migration. Knoxville, Chattanooga, Roanoke, and many of the region's smaller cities are located in the valley area, and the economic opportunities provided by these centers have promoted population concentration. Nevertheless, the region's major cities still had net migration losses during the decade. Net migration from the Blue Ridge area was approximately minus 14 percent for both the 1940–1950 and the 1950–1960 decades.[7] This figure was between the rates for the Great Valley and for the plateau region.

[1] James S. Brown and George A. Hillery, Jr., "The Great Migration, 1940-1960," *SAR*, 54-78.

[2] See Howard W. Beers, *Mobility of Rural Population: A Study of the Changes in Residence and Occupation in Two Types of Rural Communities*, Kentucky Agricultural Experiment Station Bulletin 505 (Lexington, 1947); *Effects of War on Farm Populations in Kentucky*, Kentucky Agricultural Experiment Station Bulletin 456 (Lexington, 1944); Wayne T. Gray, "Population Movements in the Kentucky Mountains," *Rural Sociology*, X (Dec. 1945), 380-86; Homer L. Hitt, "Migration between the South and Other Regions, 1949 to 1950," *Social Forces*, XXXVI (Oct. 1957), 9-16; Olaf F. Larson, "Wartime Migration and the Manpower Reserve on Farms in Eastern Kentucky," *Rural Sociology*, VIII (June 1943), 148-61; James S. Brown, "Tables Showing Components of Population Change and Percent Due to Net Migration for State Economic Areas, Metropolitan Areas, and Counties, Southern Appalachians, 1950-1960," University of Kentucky Dept. of Rural Sociology, RS-8, 1960 (unpublished data); and Roscoe Giffin, "Appalachian Newcomers in Cincinnati," *SAR*, 79-84.

[3] Brown and Hillery, "The Great Migration," *SAR*, 58.

[4] *Ibid.*, 56-57.

[5] *Ibid.*, 58.

[6] Gordon F. De Jong, *The Population of Kentucky: Changes in the Number of Inhabitants, 1950-1960* (Lexington: Kentucky Agricultural Experiment Station Bulletin 675, 1961), 12. Even though corrected for errors, the size of the rate makes it somewhat suspect of poor statistics.

[7] Brown and Hillery, "The Great Migration," *SAR*, 58.

The primary interest at this point is the effects that the out-migration from Appalachia have exerted upon fertility decline through the alteration of the age structure. The basic hypothesis is that marked long-term out-migration, particularly out-migration that is selective of young women, affects the birth rate by reducing the number of women in the childbearing age groups. In the United States the effect is more likely to be noted in a rural setting, and rural sociologists seem to be most closely attuned to this essentially demographic problem. The findings of a few studies document this research perspective.

In a careful analysis of 1940–1950 net migration and crude birth rates for the North Central states Jehlik found that areas of net in-migration showed an increase of 7.2 births per 1,000 population while areas with net out-migration had an increase of only 4.6 births per 1,000 population.[8] Glynn found the same type of relationship in a study of Texas counties.[9] His hypothesis, which was strongly supported, was that the higher the net in-migration rate of a county for the 1950–1960 decade, the smaller the decrease in the crude birth rate. Wakeley used a similar comparative design in a study of population decline in southern Illinois counties.[10] Basing his study on the general proposition that migration affects birth rates by changing the number of persons in the childbearing ages, he found that fertility ratios for high out-migration counties generally were above the average in 1940 and 1950 but below the average in 1960. The important similarity in these studies is the association of out-migration and a lower birth rate.[11]

[8] Paul J. Jehlik, "Patterns of Net Migration and Changes in Crude Birth Rates in the North Central States, 1940-1950," *Rural Sociology,* XX (Sept.-Dec. 1962), 282-88.

[9] Jerome Glynn, "Some Effects of Migration on Texas Counties, 1950-1960," *Texas Health Bulletin,* Texas Dept. of Health (Austin, April 1962), 12-17.

[10] Ray E. Wakeley, *Population Changes and Prospects in Southern Illinois.* Southern Illinois University Area Service Bulletin 1 (Carbondale, Ill., 1962), 28-31.

[11] Also see T. J. Woofter, Jr., "Trends in Rural and Urban Fertility Rates," *Rural Sociology,* XIII (March 1948), 3-9; and Rupert B. Vance, *All These People* (Chapel Hill: University of North Carolina Press, 1945), 99-100.

An assumption made in these investigations as well as the present study is that migration, especially rural-urban migration, is selective of young people. This seems to be a fairly safe assumption in light of past research. Most notable is the evidence from the studies by Thomas,[12] but many other international and United States studies have reported an age selectivity of migration.[13] Bowles, probing one step further, found that migration from farms is selective not only of young adults but particularly of young women.[14] This finding is especially significant for the present research. Brown and Hillery's investigation of Southern Appalachian Region migration is also relevant. They found that the age group of eighteen to thirty-four years comprised more than one-half of the 1949-1950 migrants from the region.[15]

In choosing a research design to investigate the effects of migration on fertility, one must consider several methodological issues. Assuming that the age and sex data for Appalachian counties are accurate, one can approach the question by estimating the age and sex distribution of migrants from each

[12] Dorothy S. Thomas, "Selective Migration," *Milbank Memorial Fund Quarterly*, XVI (Oct. 1938), 403-407; "Age and Economic Differentials in Interstate Migration," *Population Index*, XXIV (Oct. 1958), 313-25; "Age and Economic Differentials in Internal Migration in the United States: Structure and Distance," *International Union for the Scientific Study of Population* (Vienna, 1959), 714-21.

[13] See Lowry Nelson, "Selectivity of Migration from Minnesota Farms," *Proceedings of the Minnesota Academy of Science*, XVI-XVIII (1948-1950), 44-52; Edmund deS. Brunner, "Internal Migration in the United States, 1935-40," *Rural Sociology*, XIII (March 1948), 9-22; C. Horace Hamilton, "The Annual Rate of Departure of Rural Youths from Their Parental Homes," *Rural Sociology*, I (June 1936), 164-79; Warren S. Thompson, *Migration within Ohio, 1935-40* (Oxford, Ohio: Scripps Foundation for Research in Population Problems, Miami University, 1951), 105-37; Margaret Jarman Hagood and Emmit F. Sharp, *Rural-Urban Migration in Wisconsin, 1940-1950*, Wisconsin Agricultural Experiment Station Research Bulletin 176 (Madison, 1951); E. P. Hutchinson, "Internal Migration and Tuberculosis Mortality in Sweden," *American Sociological Review*, I (April 1936), 273-85; Irene B. Taeuber, "Migration and the Population Potential of Monsoon Asia," *Milbank Memorial Fund Quarterly*, XXV (Jan. 1947), 21-43; United Nations, *Sex and Age of International Migrants: Statistics for 1918-47*, ST/SOA/Series A/ 11, Population Studies (New York, 1953).

[14] Gladys K. Bowles, "Migration Patterns of the Rural Farm Population, Thirteen Economic Regions of the United States, 1940-50," *Rural Sociology*, XXII (March 1957), 1-11.

[15] Brown and Hillery, "The Great Migration," *SAR*, 67.

8

56 *Appalachian Fertility Decline*

county during the several decades. An estimate of the effect of out-migration on fertility could be obtained by applying age-specific county fertility rates to the migrant female population. It would be necessary to assume that the fertility rates of the out-migrants were identical to the fertility rates of women of the same age who remained in Appalachia. This is not a very thorough approach, because age-specific fertility rates for small units such as counties are not available. The substitution of state or national rates would provide a gross estimate of the number of births that could be attributed to the migrant female population of each county. Nevertheless, it would be difficult to arrive at conclusions about the effects of migration on the fertility rate because of the necessity of assuming equal fertility among migrant and nonmigrant females.

Another way for ascertaining the effect of migration on fertility decline is by computing product-moment correlations between decade to decade county net migration rates and changes in county fertility rates. Unlike the previous design, this approach makes possible statements about the effects of migration on fertility rates. The latter approach will be emphasized in this analysis, since a major interest is the change in rates. But also considered will be the decline in births attributable to the net out-migration of females during the 1950–1960 decade—the decade of the most rapid change.

DEFINITION OF MIGRATION

From a sociological perspective migration refers to the "shifting of an individual or a group of individuals from one relatively stable set of normative patterns of behavior (norms governing institutionalized ways of acting in a given specific social situation) to another."[16] Distance is important because people usually participate in the social interaction systems of a fairly limited area. However, a short-distance move may

[16] James S. Brown, Harry K. Schwarzweller, and Joseph J. Mangalam, "Kentucky Mountain Migration and the Stem-family: An American Variation on a Theme by Le Play," *Rural Sociology*, XXVIII (March 1963), 48-69.

involve an extensive change in social structure and social interactions. An example is a move of only a few blocks in a densely settled section of a city. The converse may also be true, as Brown, Schwarzweller, and Mangalam have pointed out in their study of eastern Kentucky migrants to southern Ohio.[17] In this case the newcomers tended to move in with family or friends who came from Kentucky. In many ways, then, the most recent arrivals operated within the same general normative order and perhaps even within a similar interaction system as before.

A major difficulty involved with the sociological concept of migration is making it operational. This problem has led most researchers to adopt the census conception of migration, which is based on a change of residence involving the crossing of a political boundary, usually a county line. Obviously, this may not coincide with the sociological concept of migration.

As used here, migration refers to the difference between out-migration and in-migration of a county for a given time period. It may be expressed in terms of the demographic equation: $M = I - E = P_2 - P_1 - (B - D)$, where M is net migration; I the number of in-migrants; E the number of out-migrants; P_2 the population at the end of the period; P_1 the population at the beginning of the period; B the number of births; and D the number of deaths. Net migration rates for Southern Appalachian counties for the 1940–1950 and 1950–1960 decades were obtained from a study by Brown and George.[18] The 1940–1960 period was chosen for study not only because of the unavailability of net migration data for prior decades, but also because it was during this period that the fertility rates of the region markedly declined.

[17] *Ibid.*, 48-69; Harry K. Schwarzweller and James S. Brown, "Education as a Cultural Bridge between Eastern Kentucky and the Great Society," *Rural Sociology*, XXVII (Dec. 1962), 357-73.

[18] James S. Brown and K. M. George, "Components of Population Change, Southern Appalachians, 1940-50 and 1950-60: Estimates of Net Migration and Natural Increase for Each Metropolitan Area, State Economic Area, and County," University of Kentucky Dept. of Rural Sociology (unpublished data). The net migration measure contains many residual errors, some of which are known and some unknown. The authors have made some adjustments for underregistration of births and infant deaths so that these errors have been reduced.

The hypothesized relationship between migration and fertility can now be stated in more precise terms: The 1940–1950 and 1950–1960 changes in county crude birth rates, fertility ratios, and general fertility rates are positively correlated to the net migration rates for comparable time periods. Net migration rates and changes in the standardized general fertility rates are not expected to be significantly correlated. The hypothesis for the standardized general fertility rate is different from the one for the other measures of fertility, since the main influence of migration on fertility is through the changes effected in age composition. When age composition is statistically controlled through standardization procedures, the effects of migration are expected to be virtually eliminated. Product-moment correlations between county net migration rates for the decades 1940–1950 and 1950–1960 and the absolute and the percentage changes in each of the four fertility measures are shown in Table 17.

The major findings can be summarized briefly. First, fertility change was more highly associated with net migration for the period 1950 to 1960 than for 1940 to 1950 on all measures except the standardized general fertility rate, the only measure for which the correlation coefficients were not statistically significant (Table 17). The direction of the association in both decades was positive; that is, the higher the net migration rate, the greater the change in fertility. This was true for net in-migration, where fertility tended to increase, as well as for net out-migration. For the entire region, however, a more accurate description would be that the greater the net migration loss, the greater the fertility decline.

Second, even though the hypothesized association was found to exist, the degree of association was lower than had been originally anticipated. The highest correlation coefficient (.44) was between the absolute decline in fertility ratios from 1950 to 1960 and the net migration rate during that decade. Thus, less than 20 percent ($.44^2$) of the variation of the fertility measure most affected was accounted for by the net migration rate. When the percentage change in the fertility ratio was used instead of the absolute change,

TABLE 17

Correlations of Absolute and Percentage Changes in Fertility Measures with Net Migration Rates for Southern Appalachian Counties, 1940–1950 and 1950–1960

Fertility Measure	CORRELATIONS OF ABSOLUTE CHANGE		CORRELATIONS OF PERCENTAGE CHANGE	
	1940–1950	1950–1960	1940–1950	1950–1960
Crude birth rate	.27[a]	.36[a]	.26[a]	.26[a]
Fertility ratio	.24[a]	.44[a]	.39[a]	.39[a]
General fertility rate	.19[a]	.24[a]	.20[a]	.17[b]
Standardized general fertility rate	.13	.06	—	—

[a] Pearsonian coefficient of correlation significant at the .01 level.
[b] Pearsonian coefficient of correlation significant at the .05 level.

the coefficient dropped to .39, still the highest for any of the fertility measures.

A third feature of the correlation analysis is that, with one exception, correlation coefficients based on changes in the fertility ratio were higher than correlation coefficients based on changes in the crude birth rate. The exception was for the 1940–1950 decade, when absolute changes in the crude birth rate were to a slight degree more highly associated with net migration. The selectivity of migration explains the higher correlations between net migration rates and changes in the fertility ratio. The crude birth rate, based on the total population, includes not only the middle-aged groups but also the young and older groups. The fertility ratio, on the other hand, is based on the women aged fifteen to forty-four years, the young-adult age group that makes up a disproportionately large part of the migration streams. As a consequence, changes in the fertility ratio tend to be more sensitive to the variations in migration.

A smaller degree of association was found between migration rates and changes in the general fertility rates. Nevertheless, the relationship is statistically significant. As expected, there was little association between migration and the standardized general fertility rate.

The statistics show a difference between correlations of the absolute change in fertility rates with net migration rates and correlations of the percentage change in the fertility rates with net migration rates. An example of a large discrepancy is the 1950–1960 change in the crude birth rate. The correlation between the absolute changes in the crude birth rate and net migration rates was .36, compared to a correlation of .26 between the percentage changes in the crude birth rate and the net migration rates. An examination of county data (Appendix A) reveals the reason for this difference. Counties with a marked decline in the crude birth rate during the 1950–1960 decade were primarily the more rural counties of the region. These counties also tended to have high birth rates in 1950. With the high 1950 rate as a base for percentage calculations the decline appeared relatively smaller than the absolute decline.

The case is almost reversed for the 1940–1950 data. Here the correlation between the percentage changes in the fertility ratio and the net migration rates was .39, and the comparable correlation between absolute changes in the fertility ratio and net migration rates was only .24. During the 1940–1950 decade the fertility ratio increased in the Southern Appalachian Region. The increase was most notable for the more urban counties, which tended to have a net migration increase during this period. With the relatively low 1940 rates as a base for the percentage calculations the percentage change in the fertility ratios appeared greater than the corresponding figures for absolute change.

The effect of net migration on the decline of fertility can be tested in another way. Standardization is the statistical procedure used to control age-structure variations, which for Southern Appalachian counties primarily result from migration. Thus, for counties with extensive migration one would expect to find considerable differences between the standardized and unstandardized general fertility rates. In order to test whether a significant number of counties had such differences the 190 Southern Appalachian Region counties were divided into three groups; first based on the standardized rate and second based on the unstandardized rate for the 1950–1960 decade. These classifications were (a) counties in which the fertility rate was equal to or less than the national rate in both 1950 and 1960 (low fertility); (b) counties in which the fertility rate was equal to or less than the national rate in 1960 but not in 1950 (changing fertility); (c) counties in which the fertility rate was above the national rate in both 1950 and 1960 (high fertility).[19]

The effect of net migration can be tested by using the null hypothesis that there is no significant difference, as measured by Chi-square, between the divisions of counties according to the standardized general fertility rate and the divisions according to the unstandardized general fertility rate. If alteration in the age structure through migration has an in-

[19] Another logically possible but unlikely pattern is one in which the general fertility rate was equal to or less than the national rate in 1950 but not in 1960.

Appalachian Fertility Decline

fluence on fertility rates, the expectation is that there will be a larger number of counties in the high fertility category with the standardized rate than with the unstandardized rate used as a basis for the ranking.[20] When the county age structures are standardized, fertility rates appear to be higher in counties that have had sizable losses of population through migration.

TABLE 18

Number of Southern Appalachian Counties with High, Changing, and Low Fertility as Classified by Unstandardized and Standardized General Fertility Rates, 1950–1960

1950–1960 Pattern	Unstandardized	Standardized
Low Fertility	10	11
Changing Fertility	95	82
High Fertility	85	97
$N = 190$ counties	$\chi^2 = 1.74$ $.10 > p > .05$	

Table 18 shows that the influence of migration on the decline of county fertility rates to the national level was not sufficiently great to merit rejection of the null hypothesis. However, the expected pattern of a larger number of counties in the high fertility category with the standardized than the unstandardized rate was observed.

Another dimension of the influence of migration on fertility is the way in which migration has affected the number of births in Appalachia. How many more children would have been born in the region if there had not been a net out-migration of young women? In other words, how many births could be attributed to the women who migrated from the region? The answer provides further evidence of important demographic changes in Appalachia.

As mentioned previously, this type of analysis involves several methodological problems, making it possible to cal-

[20] The hypothesis was not tested for the 1940-1950 decade because of the very few counties with standardized or unstandardized general fertility rates equal to or lower than the national rate.

culate only a gross estimate of the number of births attributable to the net out-migration female population. The estimate is restricted to the 1950–1960 decade for which net migration data by age, sex, and race have been published.[21] The estimate was obtained by applying age-specific fertility rates for native white women in the United States to the age-specific. net migration data for each county. Mid-decade (1955) U.S. rates were used, because age-specific county fertility rates were not available, and the average age-specific rates for Appalachian states in 1955 approximated the national rate.

If it is assumed that migration was fairly equal for each year during the 1950–1960 period, the data indicate that about 290,000 births can be attributed to the out-migrant female population. These data are significant, because during the 1950s the region's total population declined by 160,000 persons. The effect of net out-migration was not only to directly reduce the size of the population but also to reduce the size of the next generation.

CHANGING RESIDENCE PATTERNS AND FERTILITY

In addition to migration to and from the Southern Appalachian Region, changing residential patterns within the region also affect fertility. Of the thirteen counties in the region with standardized general fertility rates equal to or less than the national rate in 1960, six either contained large cities or were adjacent to urban counties. Most of the other low fertility counties contained smaller cities. The greatest proportion of low fertility counties were located in the Great Valley,[22] the section of greatest urbanization and economic development.[23] The pattern of lower fertility in urban areas fits the findings of many demographic studies in the United States and in

[21] Gladys K. Bowles and James D. Tarver, *Net Migration of the Population, 1950-60, by Age, Sex, and Color,* U.S. Dept. of Agriculture No. I, parts 3 and 4 (May 1965).

[22] John C. Belcher, "Population Growth and Characteristics," *SAR,* 39-43.

[23] Charles L. Quittmeyer and Lorin A. Thompson, "The Development of Manufacturing," *SAR,* 123-35.

other countries which have documented the rural-urban fertility differential.[24]

To the extent that urbanization and industrialization go hand-in-hand, fertility change can be considered within the framework of the theory of demographic transition which identifies three basic stages of demographic change. The first stage, typifying nonindustrial rural societies, is characterized by a high birth rate but also a high death rate. The result is a low rate of natural increase in population. Cultural patterns sanctioning high fertility are functional necessities if the population is to be maintained. The norms favoring high fertility do more than just offset high mortality, however, as they also function to provide a large labor force to enhance production in the agrarian economic system.

Industrial development and urbanization precipitate a transitional stage in which the former relative balance between birth and death rates is broken. Typically, death rates decline more rapidly than do birth rates. In part, this is true because the desire to control death is universally valued and can be greatly aided by public measures to control sanitation and health, as well as by medical practices. Birth rates, however, are not as amenable to induced change, and the

[24] See Ralph Thomlinson, *Population Dynamics* (New York: Random House, 1965), 183-84; T. Lynn Smith, *Fundamentals of Population Study* (New York: J. B. Lippincott, 1960), 308-26; Wilson H. Grabill, Clyde V. Kiser, and Pascal K. Whelpton, *The Fertility of American Women* (New York: John Wiley, 1958); Bernard Okum, *Trends in Birth Rates in the United States since 1870* (Baltimore: The Johns Hopkins Press, 1958); Abram J. Jaffe, "Urbanization and Fertility," *American Journal of Sociology*, XLVIII (July 1942), 50; P. A. Sorokin and Carle C. Zimmerman, *Principles of Rural-Urban Sociology* (New York: Henry Holt, 1929), 205-20; Otis Dudley Duncan, "Fertility of the Village Population in Pennsylvania, 1940," *Social Forces*, XXVIII (March 1950), 304-309; E. G. Flittie, "Fertility and Mortality in the Rocky Mountain West," *American Sociological Review*, XXII (April 1957), 189-93; Nathan Keyfitz, "Differential Fertility in Ontario: Application of Factorial Design to Demographic Problems," *Population Studies*, VI (Nov. 1952), 123-34; Warren C. Robinson, "Urban-Rural Differences in Indian Fertility," *Population Studies*, XIV (March 1961), 218-34; R. G. Burnight, N. L. Whetten, and B. D. Waxman, "Differential Rural-Urban Fertility in Mexico," *American Sociological Review*, XXI (Feb. 1956), 3-8; K. Bjerke, "The Birth Rate of the Rural and Urban Population in Denmark, Finland, Norway, and Sweden during the 1940's," *Proceedings of the World Population Conference, 1954*, I (New York: United Nations), 563-85.

cultural norms supporting high fertility tend to linger. The usual result is a rapid population increase—frequently so large that it negates the goals of economic development.

The third stage, typical of urban industrial societies, restores a relative balance between birth and death rates. However, unlike the first stage where birth and death rates were high, both rates are relatively low. The important difference, of course, is the decline in the birth rate, which is indicative of a complex of personal and social factors precipitating fertility control.

A major part of the world's population today resides in "developing" nations that are in the transitional stage. For these nations the major demographic problem is basically the same—the continuance of high birth rates. The demographic and sociological setting in the latter two stages of the transitional theory seems to be applicable to fertility differences within the Appalachians. Appalachia has been an area of traditionally high fertility, but it also is an area in which recent declines in fertility have altered traditional patterns. In addition, the Appalachian area remains largely rural, although this too is changing.

The two major research questions related to residence and fertility are: First, are there differences in fertility between rural and urban areas of the Southern Appalachians? Second, have there been changes in residential patterns of the Southern Appalachian population that are related to the decline in fertility? An analysis of residence patterns and population change in relation to differing fertility patterns will help to answer these questions. This consideration will use the previously discussed classification of counties on the basis of 1950 and 1960 fertility rates.

The residence categories used in this analysis follow the census definitions of Standard Metropolitan Areas, urban areas, and rural areas. Basically, a metropolitan area is a county or group of contiguous counties that contains at least one city of 50,000 inhabitants or more. Urban areas are places of 2,500 persons or more which are outside metropolitan areas. The remaining villages and open country areas are classified as rural.

Table 19, which presents the 1960 residential patterns of

the Southern Appalachian Region within each pattern of county fertility change, reveals a pronounced relationship between residence and fertility patterns. Metropolitan areas tended to have low fertility, while rural areas tended to have high fertility. More than 70 percent of the Appalachian population living in counties with low fertility rates were classified as metropolitan residents, while more than 76 percent of those living in high fertility areas were rural residents. In fact, less than 3 percent of the population living in high fertility counties were metropolitan residents.

TABLE 19

Residence in Low, Changing, and High Fertility Counties, Southern Appalachian Region Population, 1960

County Fertility Type	Rural	Urban	Metropolitan	Total
Low	16.4	12.6	71.0	100.0
Changing	60.2	15.5	24.3	100.0
High	76.4	21.1	2.6	100.0
Total	58.3	17.2	24.5	100.0

SOURCE: *U.S. Census of Population, 1960.*

The data demonstrate another interesting point. More than 60 percent of the population living in counties in which the fertility rate decline to the national level during the 1950–1960 decade were classified as rural. Thus, the decline of fertility was not restricted to urban and metropolitan areas. This limits the importance that might be attached to urban and metropolitan residence and suggests that other factors are also influencing fertility patterns.

The next consideration is: Have there been changes in residential patterns of the Southern Appalachian population that are related to the decline in fertility? Theoretically, a disproportional population increase in urban and metropolitan areas would support an affirmative response. In general, the data in Table 20 support the conclusion that changes in residential patterns are correlated with fertility changes. The increase in urban or metropolitan residence was noted espe-

TABLE 20

Percentage Change in the Population Classified as Rural, Urban, and Metropolitan for the Southern Appalachian Region, 1950–1960[a]

County Fertility Type	Rural	Urban	Metropolitan	Total
Low	− 5.2	5.0	12.8	8.4
Changing	− 1.3	− 0.6	4.9	0.2
High	−14.8	12.4	1.1	−9.9
Total Change	− 9.2	6.3	9.0	−2.8

SOURCE: *U.S. Census of Population, 1960.*

[a] For comparative purposes, Fayette County, W. Va., was not classified as a metropolitan area in 1950.

cially in both low and high fertility areas. Although this increase might have been expected in low fertility areas, the change toward urban and metropolitan residence in high fertility areas indicates that shifts in the residential patterns alone may not assure low fertility. Of course, high fertility areas remained predominantly rural (Table 19). In counties classified as changing fertility areas the shift toward increased urban or metropolitan residence was less marked.

The question which rather naturally follows concerns what there is about rural and urban residence that influences this frequently noted fertility differential,[25] particularly the fertility differential in the Southern Appalachians. Though the more urban areas of the region have birth rates below the national average, many of the more rural mountain counties retain the pattern of high fertility. Certainly the rural-urban

[25] See John F. Kantner and Pascal K. Whelpton, "Fertility Rates and Fertility Planning by Character of Migration," *Milbank Memorial Fund Quarterly*, XXX (April 1952), 152-87; Clyde V. Kiser, "Fertility Rates in the United States by Residence and Migration," *Proceedings, International Population Conference* (Vienna, 1959), 273-86; David Goldberg, "The Fertility of Two Generation Urbanites," *Population Studies*, XII (March 1959), 214-22; Ronald Freedman and Doris Slesinger, "Fertility Differentials for the Indigenous Nonfarm Population of the United States," *Population Studies*, XV (Nov. 1961), 161-73; Charles F. Westoff, Robert G. Potter, Jr., Philip Sagi, and Elliot G. Mishler, *Family Growth in Metropolitan America* (Princeton: Princeton University Press, 1961), 263-81.

differential is not just a matter of changes in longitude and latitude.

One important factor is the differing social characteristics of rural and urban populations. Urban residents tend to have higher education levels and incomes, and these variables are associated with lower birth rates. There is, however, nothing magical about an increased education or greater income that precludes a large family.[26]

There also tend to be rural-urban differences in the status of women. Women residing in urban areas are more likely to fulfill roles other than those of housewife and mother. Perhaps this is particularly true in Appalachia, where vestiges of masculine dominance and the patriarchal family system are still evident. And, if generalizations can be made from another study of fertility among people with a similar family system, one of the consequences that this system has for fertility is the general lack of communication between husband and wife regarding fertility and sex attitudes.[27]

Another factor in rural-urban fertility difference is that in areas such as rural Appalachia the cost of rearing a child is not as great as it is in an urban setting. A large family may not be considered an economic liability; rather, children may be able to assist in farmwork and other activities that augment production and income. In many circumstances, some food products are produced at home. Pressures that come with social mobility and the middle-class style of life, which absorb much of the energies and resources of urban residents in the United States, are not as dominant in Southern Appalachia. These factors are closely tied to levels of education, socioeconomic status, occupation, and income.

Compared to urban areas age at marriage tends to be lower in rural areas, particularly in the rural areas of the Appalachians.[28] A younger age at marriage helps to keep fertility high by lengthening the time period that women are exposed

---

[26] J. V. D. Saunders, *Differential Fertility in Brazil* (Gainesville: University of Florida Press, 1958).

[27] Lee Rainwater, *And the Poor Get Children* (Chicago: Quadrangle Books, 1960).

[28] Vance, *All These People*, 95-108; and T. S. Hyland, "The Fruitful Mountaineer," *Life*, XXVII (Dec. 26, 1949), 66.

to childbearing. Coupled with the younger age of marriage, Vance found the likelihood that people in the Appalachians eventually would marry was greater than that for the U.S. population as a whole.[29]

Although there are additional factors that contribute to rural-urban fertility differences, a general mosaic begins to appear. The differences reflect the varying ways that people live, and the rural-urban dimension is a valuable index of many other sociological and social psychological factors. However, while rural-urban differences have considerable predictive value, mere differences in the way people live can hardly explain fertility change.[30] Insight into the dynamics of change can be obtained, however, by exploring people's attitudes and values about fertility and family size.

[29] *Ibid.*
[30] William Petersen, *Population* (New York: Macmillan, 1961), 214-32.

4. *Attitudes*

The transition to the smaller family system, which has accompanied the transformation from a rural to an urban society, has been a complex change. The change has involved largely unsystematized complexes of attitudes and values that underlie basic elements of human behavior. This chapter analyzes opinion responses to questions about fertility that were designed to provide insights into the attitude and value complexes of Southern Appalachian residents.

This investigation is primarily an exploratory study of the attitudes and values of respondents who live in counties where fertility is declining toward national levels, but where net out-migration does not appear to account for all of the change. The basic research question is: Have there been changes in the attitudes and values of the region's residents that are in part responsible for the decline in fertility? Unfortunately, this question cannot be answered directly, since data are available for only one time period. A thorough study of sociological and social psychological factors associated with declining fertility would employ a panel or longitudinal research design. Some of the undesirable characteristics of the *post hoc* design can be reduced, however, by employing an alternate plan for investigating "causal influence" suggested by Nagel.[1] In this type of investigation experimental manipulation is on the recorded data about given factors. The factors themselves would be the objects of experimental manipulation in a longitudinal design. In the present case available data on fertility are manipulated to simulate fertility change over time. This model can be applied to fertility change in the Appalachians, using the previously outlined groupings of counties based on 1950–1960 fertility patterns. This approach makes possible a study of attitude and value change by a consideration of the problem from the perspective of whether or not Southern Appalachian Region respondents living in high, changing, and low fertility areas have similar or different opinions about fertility. If the responses are different, the analysis can determine if they make sense in terms of fertility change: that is, do respondents living in high fertility areas hold opinions that are most indicative of high fertility behavior and low fertility area respondents of low fertility?

The comparisons are for ecological units, not individuals, whose attitudes obviously may vary from that of the entire group. Prior studies have shown that it is tenuous to move from ecological relationships, such as those between various rates, to relationships between individuals.[2] Although caution must be maintained, the present analysis is somewhat different from some research in that the relationships studied are not between rates but between opinion-response patterns of individuals living in different areas of the Appalachians. It is analogous to comparing voting-preference statements of people living in different areas of the country, or to comparing the responses of rural and urban residents to a question about foreign aid. It is also important to recognize that the ecological units, which are based on county fertility change patterns, are not necessarily sequential. Response patterns of individuals living in low fertility areas may not be simply a later version of the response patterns of those living in changing fertility areas. Nevertheless, this method of analysis may suggest important factors in fertility decline—factors that are functions of common underlying perspectives inherent not in the individual but in interindividual differences and relationships.[3]

An unusual feature of the study design is the grouping of respondents on the basis of the dependent variable—fertility. The usual procedure is to group respondents on some independent or control variable. This leads to the question of

[1] Ernest Nagel, *The Structure of Science* (New York: Harcourt, Brace, and World, 1961), 450-59.

[2] W. S. Robinson, "Ecological Correlations and the Behavior of Individuals," *American Sociological Review*, XV (June 1950), 351-57.

[3] Herbert Menzel, "Comments on Robinson's 'Ecological Correlations and the Behavior of Individuals,'" *American Sociological Review*, XV (Oct. 1950), 674.

whether or not the responses to opinion questions about fertility are by definition related to the county fertility change patterns. Or, stated another way, is the study tautological? There are several reasons why this is not the case. First, and perhaps most important, is the logical jump between an opinion statement and the complementary behavior. While a discrepancy in these two components is noted in many types of research, it is especially true in fertility research where the link between, for instance, an opinion about ideal family size and the actual number of children born is complicated by numerous biological, psychological, economic, and sociological factors.

This study was designed to tap generalized attitudes and values concerning fertility and family size rather than to elicit specific opinions about the respondent's own family situation. For example, the question about ideal family size was worded: "What do you think is the ideal number of children for the average young couple starting out married life today?" Despite this careful wording in terms of a generalized ideal, a doubt remains about whether the actual number of children the respondent has does tend to become the same number, or very close to the same number, given in his reply.

Some empirical evidence on this point is provided in findings from the Growth of the American Family study, which was based on a nationwide sample of married couples. For the total sample, including respondents of three major religious groups (Protestants, Catholics, and Jews), the mean number of children that respondents considered ideal for all American families differed significantly from the mean number of children that they considered ideal for their own family.[4] In fact, the generalized ideal differed from both the current mean family size and the mean number of children expected. Protestant respondents, for example, considered a mean family size of 3.4 children to be ideal for all Americans; but the mean number of children they desired them-

[4] Ronald Freedman, Pascal K. Whelpton, and John W. Smit, "Socio-Economic Factors in Religious Differentials in Fertility," *American Sociological Review*, XXVI (Aug. 1961), 608-14.

selves was 3.0; the mean expected number of births when their family is completed was 2.9; and the mean number of births at the time of the interview was 2.1. Data for Catholic and Jewish respondents showed similar differences, and these differences were found to persist when respondents in the three religious groups were matched on the basis of occupation, education, income, duration of marriage, residence, and farm or nonfarm background. In sum, the evidence suggests that the respondents perceived the question about the ideal family size for Americans as different from their personal desires and expectations about family size, as well as from actual number of children that they had.

The assumption underlying the present analysis is that the direction of causal inference is from attitudes and values to actual fertility. However, since manipulative control of these variables is lacking in the research design, it is well to recognize that a reverse relationship is also possible. The goal here is merely to determine the presence or absence of a correlation. With fertility research in its current stage of development one cannot *assume* a direct relationship between verbal response and behavior.

Another important factor that avoids a tautological relationship between the independent and dependent variables is the opposite way in which migration and changes in attitudes about fertility would be expected to affect the county fertility groupings. The county fertility groupings were based on empirical observations of fertility change. Migration's primary influence on fertility change is in changing the proportion of persons in the population who are in the childbearing ages. The greatest influence of migration, then, would be expected in rural areas, where the out-migration is heaviest. On the other hand, changes in attitudes and values would be expected to exert primary influence on fertility change in metropolitan areas. As a result, the observed changes in county fertility patterns cannot *a priori* be attributed to a single factor.

Another possibility is that any relationship that may exist between fertility attitudes and county fertility types is a function of personal and social characteristics of the respondents (for instance, age or socioeconomic status). This point will be analyzed in some detail in the next chapter.

The data for this phase of the study were collected as part of a sample survey financed by the Ford Foundation of respondents living in Southern Appalachian Region households. The execution of the survey was the responsibility of the University of North Carolina's Survey Operations Unit. This unit defined the universe for the household survey as a seven-state, 190-county area, including portions of Kentucky, Tennessee, Alabama, Georgia, North Carolina, Virginia, and West Virginia. The design was a stratified two-stage sample. Three strata were chosen—rural, urban, and Standard Metropolitan Area. Four hundred localities in sixty-nine counties of the area were selected in which to conduct interviews. The sample included 1,466 households with a sampling error of 6.0 percent—low for this type of sample. Of the 1,466 households, 1,412 were white households, and these constitute the sample to be investigated in this study.

The responses to six questions will be used in analyzing whether household respondents living in different fertility areas had similar or differing attitudes and values about fertility. The opinion responses can be seen as indicating different aspects of the complex of attitudes and values that compose the underlying structure of fertility behavior. Included are items about ideal family size, ideal age at marriage, and opinions about birth control practices for married couples.

At this point it might be well to indicate briefly how the terms attitudes and values are used in this research.[5] As Davis and Williams have written, a significant quality of values is their inferential character. Williams defines values operationally as "overt choice or preference, as attention or emphasis, as statement or assertion. . . . These various evidences are 'pointers' that say 'this is what is meant.'" Attitudes are usually considered to be more specific than values; however, the inferential quality is common to both. The

[5] Much of the discussion of attitudes and values is based on George A. Hillery, Jr., "Felt Population Pressures in India: Methods of Identification," *Population Review*, V (July 1961), 41-49.

primary importance of the concept linkage between attitudes and values is the broader scope of data made available to the study of values.[6] The base component of attitude and value studies is a wide range of opinion statements related to the subject area. It is by means of opinion statements that the Southern Appalachian Survey data provide information on respondents' attitudes and values about fertility.

IDEAL FAMILY SIZE

(One of the many possible facets of fertility attitudes and values is the respondents' beliefs about ideal family size.) The question asked sought a picture of the stereotyped impressions of what the ideal family size should be.

(For all respondents in the Southern Appalachian survey a median of 3.6 children was considered to be ideal (Table 21). However, respondents living in low, changing, and high fertility areas of the Southern Appalachian Region had different opinions about the ideal family size for the average young couple. Almost one-half of the high fertility area respondents reported a family of four children or more as ideal, compared to less than 30 percent of the low fertility area residents who reported an ideal that large. On the other hand, a higher percentage of low (40.8) than high (25.2) fertility area respondents said that an ideal family size was two children or less. The data suggest the existence of a meaningful difference for this item among respondents living in low, changing, and high fertility areas of the region.)

Since questions about ideal family size are so frequently

[6] Kingsley Davis, *Human Society* (New York: Macmillan, 1949), 124; Robin M. Williams, Jr., *American Society* (New York: Alfred A. Knopf, 1952), 376-82; see the definition given by Gordon W. Allport: a "mental and neural state of readiness, organized through experience, exerting a directive or dynamic influence upon the individual's response to all objects and situations to which it is related," "Attitudes," in *A Handbook of Social Psychology,* ed. Carl Murchison (Worcester, Mass.: Clark University Press, 1935). See also Theodore M. Newcomb, *Social Psychology* (New York: Dryden Press, 1950), 117-18; for an extensive theory of attitudes and values see Daniel Katz and Ezra Stotland, "A Preliminary Statement to a Theory of Attitudinal Structure and Change," in *Psychology: A Study of a Science,* ed. Sigmund Koch (New York: McGraw-Hill, 1959), III, 423-75.

TABLE 21

Percentage Distribution of the Number of Children Considered Ideal for the Average Young Couple, by County Fertility Type, for White Respondents in the Southern Appalachian Region, 1958

| County Fertility Type | IDEAL NUMBER OF CHILDREN | | | | |
	2 or less	3	4	5 or more	Median
Low $(N = 360)$	40.8	30.6	25.6	3.0	3.30
Changing $(N = 557)$	28.5	34.5	30.7	6.3	3.62
High $(N = 428)$	25.2	25.0	37.6	12.2	3.99
Total $(N = 1,345)$	30.8	30.4	31.5	7.3	3.63

Don't know and no response $= 67$ $\chi^2 = 56.94$ $p < .001$

used as measures of desired fertility, it is interesting to compare the results of the present study with those of other studies. Differences in sample populations, wording of questions, summary statistics, and perhaps cultural interpretations make exacting conclusions dangerous. However, the main interest is fitting the present research into a broader context of attitudinal studies on fertility.

As a group the Southern Appalachian Region respondents seemed to favor a larger ideal family size than did the respondents in nationwide surveys in Japan, France, and the United States (Table 22). On the other hand, Appalachian respondents favored a slightly smaller ideal family size than did respondents in Lebanon, Johannesburg, and four Japanese villages. The focusing of attention on such large groupings of people tends to obscure the internal variations which definitely exist in the Southern Appalachian Region (Table 21). It is interesting to note, however, that for the selected studies the ideal family size of the Appalachian respondents occupied a middle position in the distribution. It is possible that the opinions of Appalachian respondents concerning ideal family size may represent a transitional stage between a past era of a presumably (but not known) higher ideal family size and a future era of a lower ideal family size akin to the United States average. This, of course, follows the basic model of

TABLE 22

Comparison of the Results of Selected Studies of the Ideal Number of Children

Source	Year	Place of Study	Subjects	Summary Statistic
Yaukey	1958–1959	Lebanon	married women	Moslem 3.8–4.7 (median)
				Christian 3.8–4.1 (median)
Higgins	1957–1958	Johannesburg	white women	4.1 (median)
Dore	1950	Four Japanese villages	farmers	3.8 (mean)
De Jong (present study)	1958	Southern Appalachians	white men & women	3.63 (median)
Yeracaris	1956	Buffalo	mothers	3.63 (mean)
Freedman, Whelpton, and Campbell	1955	United States (national sample)	married white women	3.4 (mean)
Dore	1950	Japan (national sample)	adults	3.3 (mean)
Freedman and Sharp	1952	Detroit	population over 21 years	3.15 (mean)
Freedman, Goldberg, and Sharp	1954	Detroit	population over 21 years	2.94 (mean)
Girard and Henry	1955	France (national sample)	adults	2.85 (mean)

SOURCES: David Yaukey, *Fertility Differences in a Modernizing Country* (Princeton: Princeton University Press, 1961), 72-74; Edward Higgins, "Some Fertility Attitudes Among White Women in Johannesburg," *Population Studies,* XVI (July 1962), 70-78; R. P. Dore, "Japanese Rural Fertility: Some Social and Economic Factors," *Population Studies,* VII (July 1953), 62-88; Constantine A. Yeracaris, "Differentials in the Relationship Between Values and Practices in Fertility," *Social Forces,* XXXVIII (Dec. 1959), 153-58; Ronald Freedman, Pascal K. Whelpton, and Arthur A. Campbell, *Family Planning, Sterility, and Population Growth* (New York: McGraw-Hill, 1959), 222; Ronald Freedman and Harry Sharp, "Correlates of Values About Ideal Family Size in the Detroit Metropolitan Area," *Population Studies,* VIII (July 1954), 34-45; Ronald Freedman, David Goldberg, and Harry Sharp, "'Ideals' About Family Size in the Detroit Metropolitan Area: 1954," *Milbank Memorial Fund Quarterly,* XXXIII (April 1955), 187-97; Alain Girard and Louis Henry, "Les Attitudes et la Conjoncture Démographique: Natalité Structure Familiale et Limites de la Vie Active," *Population,* XI (Jan.-March 1956), 105-41.

the transitional theory, which is based on fertility rates and
not on fertility attitudes. Nevertheless, the model provides
a suggestive, although untested, frame of reference.

PERCEIVED INFLUENCE OF ECONOMIC STATUS
ON IDEAL NUMBER OF CHILDREN

Perhaps one of the most frequent observations about fertility
is its apparent tie with economic status. Some writers feel
that an increase in economic status on the personal as well
as the national level is one of the prime factors in predicting
a fertility decline.[7] Indeed, most studies of fertility and family
size contain some measure of economic status.[8])

The usual approach to the "and the poor get children"
hypothesis is to analyze the family sizes of persons of different economic strata. While this is a fruitful approach for
investigating actual family size, it is less pertinent to a discussion of attitudes about fertility. A more pertinent question
is whether or not people perceive family size to be related
to economic conditions of the family. The Southern Appalachian Survey attempted to secure an indication of the
respondents' perceptions of the influence of economic status
on attitudes about the number of children considered ideal.
Respondents were asked: (a) "What is the ideal number of
children for the well-off young couple starting out today?" and
(b) "What is the ideal number of children for the not well-off
young couple starting out today?"

[7] See Rudolf Heberle, "Social Factors in Birth Control," *American Sociological Review*, VI (Dec. 1941), 794-805; T. J. Woofter, Jr., "Factors Sustaining the Birth Rate," *American Sociological Review*, XIV (June 1949), 357-66.

[8] For example, see Charles F. Westoff, Robert G. Potter, Jr., Philip C. Sagi, and Elliot G. Mishler, *Family Growth in Metropolitan America* (Princeton: Princeton University Press, 1961); Ronald Freedman, Pascal K. Whelpton, and Arthur A. Campbell, *Family Planning, Sterility, and Population Growth* (New York: McGraw-Hill, 1959); Pascal K. Whelpton and Clyde V. Kiser, eds., *Social and Psychological Factors Affecting Fertility* (5 vols.; New York: Milbank Memorial Fund, 1946-1958); Margaret Jarman Hagood, "Changing Fertility Differentials among Farm-Operator Families in Relation to Economic Size of Farms," *Rural Sociology*, XIII (Dec. 1948), 363-73; W. Stys, "The Influence of Economic Conditions on the Fertility of Peasant Women," *Population Studies*, XI (Nov. 1957), 136-48.

The two questions tap different levels of reality. The first question in some ways indicates a "purer" attitude, since the problems of family finances are eliminated. But economic considerations are of utmost relevance in the second question. Conceivably, we have a difference between what would be considered to be the ideal family size if the respondent were wealthy and what he will do to become wealthy.

The responses to these questions were general rather than specific—they were not expressly directed to the respondent's situation. Rather, they sought the individual's impression of what the ideal family size should be under differing economic conditions. A striking feature of the data in Table 23 is the extraordinarily high family size preference when a couple is perceived to be economically well-off. For all respondents

TABLE 23

Percentage Distribution of the Number of Children Considered Ideal for the Well-Off Young Couple, by County Fertility Type, for White Respondents in the Southern Appalachian Region, 1958

County Fertility Type	IDEAL NUMBER OF CHILDREN				
	3 or less	4	5	6 or more	Median
Low ($N = 347$)	23.1	45.5	12.1	19.3	4.59
Changing ($N = 531$)	19.2	41.4	12.2	27.1	4.74
High ($N = 408$)	17.9	31.9	16.2	34.0	5.02
Total ($N = 1,286$)	19.8	39.5	13.5	27.2	4.76

Don't know and no response $= 126$ $\chi^2 = 30.74$ $p < .001$

the ideal family size preference was about five children (median of 4.76). In fact, more than one-fourth felt that six or more children was an ideal size.

Again, there was a statistically significant difference between the opinions of respondents living in low, changing, and high fertility areas. This finding is consistent with the one for the ideal family size for the average young couple. More than 50 percent of the respondents in the high fertility area designated an ideal of five children or more. By comparison, less than one-third of the respondents in low fertility areas thought five or more children was an ideal family size. With the ideal family size for an average young couple used as a base the perceived influence of a favorable economic status added about one child to the overall median ideal of Southern Appalachian Region respondents.

The responses to the second question—the ideal number of children for the not well-off couple—again support the conclusion that respondents living in low, changing, and high fertility areas held different opinions about ideal family size. However, the respondents living in areas where fertility declined to the national level in 1960 reported a lower median (2.12) as compared to respondents living in low fertility areas (2.25). Nevertheless, both groups of respondents expressed a considerably lower ideal than the respondents in high fertility areas. A possible explanation is that the low median ideal family size for respondents living in areas of declining fertility is indicative of the influence of economic status on fertility change.

For the not well-off young couple the respondents felt that approximately two children was an ideal number (Table 24). Between 85 and 90 percent of the low and changing fertility area respondents favored an ideal of two children or less,

TABLE 24

Percentage Distribution of the Number of Children Considered Ideal for the Not Well-Off Young Couple, by County Fertility Type, for White Respondents in the Southern Appalachian Region, 1958

County Fertility Type	IDEAL NUMBER OF CHILDREN				
	0	1	2	3 or more	Median
Low ($N = 352$)	14.2	23.0	52.2	10.8	2.25
Changing ($N = 550$)	23.3	11.4	51.1	14.2	2.12
High ($N = 409$)	15.2	13.2	45.2	26.4	2.48
Total ($N = 1,311$)	18.3	15.1	49.5	17.1	2.34

Don't know and no response $= 101$ $\chi^2 = 67.12$ $p < .001$

compared to about 74 percent of the respondents living in high fertility areas. For all areas a significant point is the reduction in the designated ideal family size for not well-off couples (median of 2.34) as compared to the well-off couples (median of 4.76).

By national standards a majority of Appalachian families would not be considered economically well-off. Nevertheless, fertility is still above the national average in many rural areas, even though the statements about ideal family size for a not well-off couple were rather low (Table 24). In part, this may indicate the difference between a generalized fertility ideal and actual fertility. It may also be indicative of national and Appalachian differences in the determination of what constitutes an economically deprived couple.

In comparison to the average, a well-off economic status increased the median ideal family size by approximately 1.0

TABLE 25

Perceived Influence of Economic Status on Ideal Number of Children, by County Fertility Type, for White Respondents in the Southern Appalachian Region, 1958

| Subject | County Fertility Type | | | |
	Low	Changing	High	All Types
	Approximate Difference Between Medians[a]			
Extent to which the median family size for well-off couple is above median for average couple	1.3	1.1	1.0	1.3
Extent to which the median family size for not well-off couple is below median for average couple	1.1	1.5	1.5	1.3

[a] It is realized, of couse, that exact differences between medians are largely meaningless. Unlike means, medians express position in a distribution of scores and are not as amenable to statistical manipulation. The interest here, then, is not an exact measure of increase and decrease in medians, but rather a comparison of general trends. For this purpose, differences between medians are rounded to one decimal to indicate approximations.

for the high fertility area respondents and approximately 1.3 for the low fertility area respondents, with the median for respondents in changing fertility areas occupying a middle position (Table 25). Comparison of average and not well-off economic statuses reduced the median ideal by approximately 1.1 for the low fertility area respondents. As a result, the high and changing fertility area respondents, though expressing a preference for larger families for the average couple, reported a smaller increase and a larger decrease for well-off and not well-off economic statuses, respectively, than did the low fertility area respondents. One can only speculate about whether or not this means that the high and changing fertility area respondents are more sensitive—at least on the attitudinal level—to the effects of economic status on family size.

IDEAL AGE AT MARRIAGE

One of the fertility correlates most familiar to demographers is age at marriage. Seldom has a relationship been documented with such consistency as has that of the negative correlation between age at marriage and fertility—not only in western nations but also in nonwestern countries.[9] The reason for this relationship seems fairly simple. In most cultures babies

[9] Dennis Wrong, "Trends in Class Fertility in Western Nations," *Canadian Journal of Economics and Political Science,* XXIV (May 1958), 216-29; J. F. C. Blacker, "Fertility Trends of the Asian Population of Tanganyika," *Population Studies,* XIII (July 1959), 46-60; Frederick S. Crum, "The Decadence of the Native American Stock," *Journal of the American Statistical Association,* XIV (Sept. 1914), 215-22; R. P. Dore, "Japanese Rural Fertility: Some Social and Economic Factors," *Population Studies,* VII (July 1953), 62-88; Irene B. Taeuber, "Continuities in the Declining Fertility of the Japanese," *Milbank Memorial Fund Quarterly,* XXXVIII (July 1960), 264-83; Alain Girard and Louis Henry, "Les Attitudes et la Conjoncture Démographique: Natalité Structure Familiale et Limites de la Vie Active," *Population,* XI (Jan.-March 1956), 105-41; John F. Kantner and Robert G. Potter, Jr., "The Relationship of Family Size in Two Successive Generations," *Milbank Memorial Fund Quarterly,* XXXII (July 1954), 294-311; Arnold S. Feldman and Paul K. Hatt, "Social Structure as Affecting Fertility in Puerto Rico," *Annals of the American Academy of Political and Social Sciences,* CCLXXXV (Jan. 1953), 123-29.

ordinarily are born to married couples, and marriage signals
the start of reproductive life. Age at marriage, therefore,
influences the length of time that a woman can become
pregnant.[10] There are, of course, many factors, such as birth
control, that may affect the relationship between age at marriage and fertility; nevertheless, it remains sufficiently important to warrant consideration.)

Southern Appalachian Region respondents were asked what
they considered the ideal age at marriage for a woman and
for a man. As with the other opinion questions, the analysis
of responses tested for meaningful similarities or differences
in response patterns for people living in different areas of
the Appalachians.

In line with the United States pattern Appalachian household respondents felt that a man should marry at an older
age than a woman (Tables 26 and 27). For the entire sample

TABLE 26

Percentage Distribution of Ideal Age at Marriage for a Woman,
by County Fertility Type, Given by White Respondents in the
Southern Appalachian Region, 1958

| County Fertility Type | IDEAL AGE AT MARRIAGE | | | | |
	19 and under	20	21	22 and over	Median
Low ($N = 362$)	17.7	21.5	26.2	34.6	21.4
Changing ($N = 584$)	27.4	28.6	27.1	16.9	20.8
High ($N = 443$)	40.9	31.6	17.4	10.1	20.3
Total ($N = 1,389$)	29.2	27.7	23.7	19.4	20.8

Don't know and no response $= 23$ $\chi^2 = 120.01$ $p < .001$

there was approximately a two-year difference between the
ideal median age at marriage for a man and for a woman. The
difference was greater in low fertility areas and smaller in
high fertility areas. Ideally, respondents felt that a woman

[10] Carl E. Taylor, John B. Wyon, and John E. Gordon, "Ecological
Determinants of Population Growth," *Milbank Memorial Fund Quarterly*,
XXXVI (April 1958), 117.

TABLE 27

Percentage Distribution of Ideal Age at Marriage for a Man, by County Fertility Type, Given by White Respondents in the Southern Appalachian Region, 1958

County Fertility Type	21 and under	22	23–24	25 and over	Median
Low ($N = 359$)	29.2	9.7	20.9	40.1	24.1
Changing ($N = 586$)	39.1	14.2	22.2	24.5	22.8
High ($N = 445$)	50.8	9.0	21.8	18.4	22.0
Total ($N = 1,390$)	40.3	11.4	21.7	26.6	22.8

Don't know and no response = 22 $\quad\quad \chi^2 = 67.21 \quad\quad p < .001$

should be almost twenty-one years old at marriage and a man almost twenty-three years old.

Respondents living in high fertility areas of the region favored a considerably lower age at marriage for both a woman and a man than did persons living in low fertility areas. For instance, more than 40 percent of the high fertility area respondents, compared to less than 18 percent of the low fertility area respondents, felt that a woman should be age nineteen or under at marriage. Similarly, more than one-half of the high fertility area respondents considered twenty-one or under as a man's ideal age at marriage while less than 30 percent of the low fertility area respondents held such an opinion. From the data available it appears that changes are occurring in the stereotyped Appalachian propensity for early marriages.

BIRTH CONTROL PRACTICES

Attitudes and values about birth control practices for married people are another dimension of fertility. According to Petersen, birth control practices have largely been responsible for altering the direction of fertility trends in most western nations and Japan.[11] This conclusion is supported by research

[11] William Petersen, *Population* (New York: Macmillan, 1961), 566-67.

in several nations, including western Europe, Japan, and the United States.[12] Underdeveloped nations constitute a somewhat different situation. Limits on fertility have been primarily a matter of physiological capabilities; elementary positive Malthusian checks, such as wars, famines, and epidemics; and various periods of continence associated with lactation, warfare, religion, and widowhood. It is not that attempts to limit family size are absent.[13] What is missing is the neo-Malthusian ideology that views birth control practices as socially good, leading to happier family life and improved national and personal welfare.[14]

One of the studies of contraception in the United States is Beebe's research in the Southern Appalachians.[15] A major concern of his research was the effectiveness of birth control clinics and other programs designed to encourage the use of contraceptives. Beebe recognized, however, that the effectiveness of birth control programs was largely dependent upon the participants' basic attitudes and values about birth control.

Since birth control practices are of such obvious importance in the determining of fertility trends, an attempt was made to discover Southern Appalachian respondents' attitudes about

[12] See J. Kitaoka, "How Japan Halved Her Birth Rate in Ten Years," paper presented at the Sixth International Conference on Planned Parenthood (New Delhi, 1959), as quoted in Shri R. A. Gopalaswami, "How Japan Halved Her Birth Rate in Ten Years: A Lesson for India," *Population Review*, III (July 1959), 52-57; Ronald Freedman, G. Baumert, and M. Bolte, "Expected Family Size and Family Size Values in West Germany," *Population Studies*, XIII (Nov. 1959), 136-50; Robert R. Kiczynski, "The Decrease of Fertility," *Economica*, II (May 1935), 128-41; Woofter, "Factors Sustaining the Birth Rate"; Regine K. Stix, "Research in Causes of Variations in Fertility: Medical Aspects," *American Sociological Review*, II (Oct. 1937), 668-77; Freedman, Whelpton, and Campbell, *Family Planning, Sterility, and Population Growth*.

[13] William A. Morrison, "Family Planning Attitudes of Industrial Workers of Ambarnath, a City of Western India: A Comparative Analysis," *Population Studies*, XIV (March 1961), 235-48; "Attitudes of Males toward Family Planning in a Western Indian Village," *Milbank Memorial Fund Quarterly*, XXXIV (July 1956), 262-86; J. N. Shri, "Differential Fertility and Family Limitation in an Urban Community of Uttar Pradesh," *Population Studies*, XI (Nov. 1957), 157-69.

[14] Petersen, *Population*, 566.

[15] Gilbert W. Beebe, *Conception and Fertility in the Southern Appalachians* (Baltimore: Williams and Wilkins, 1942).

these practices. Respondents were asked the questions: "What is your opinion about birth control practices for married people? Are these practices always wrong, sometimes wrong, or never wrong?" The largest proportion of respondents (about 44 percent) indicated some reservation by answering that birth control practices were "sometimes wrong" (Table 28) The remainder were almost equally divided

TABLE 28

Percentage Distribution of Opinions About Birth Control Practices For Married People, by County Fertility Type, Given by White Respondents in the Southern Appalachian Region, 1958

County Fertility Type	Always wrong	Sometimes wrong	Never wrong
Low (N = 361)	18.0	47.7	34.3
Changing (N = 571)	28.4	38.9	32.7
High (N = 418)	29.9	46.9	23.2
Total (N = 1,350)	26.1	43.7	30.2

Don't know and no response = 62 $\chi^2 = 27.90$ $p < .001$

between the "always wrong" and "never wrong" categories. As was true with all of the previously analyzed opinion statements, there was a statistically significant difference between the response patterns of people living in low, changing, and high fertility areas of the region. Almost 30 percent of the predominantly rural respondents from high fertility areas felt that it was always wrong for married people to practice birth control, while only 18 percent of the low fertility area respondents held such an opinion. Similarly, a higher proportion of the low than the high fertility area respondents considered it never wrong for married people to practice birth control.

Although the question was of a personal nature, only about 4 percent of the sample either did not have an opinion or gave no response. The diversity in the response pattern would seem to indicate that the issue is quite controversial. If this is true, the question probably is tapping a fundamental dimension of fertility attitudes.

Interestingly, a sizable majority (73.9 percent) of the region's respondents did not completely condemn birth control by married couples. Although the lack of condemnation cannot be directly equated with approval or adoption of birth control practices, it does indicate some positive orientation toward the control of family size.

While comparative data are scarce, attitudinal studies in India, Puerto Rico, South Africa, and the United States present a generalized picture of birth control values among people in other areas. Morrison, for example, found that 91 percent of the adult males in an Indian city held an unfavorable opinion toward the practice of birth control.[16] Among white married women of Johannesburg only 21 percent were unfavorable.[17] About the same proportion (26 percent) of Southern Appalachian Region respondents were very unfavorable. In Puerto Rico 12.5 percent of the adult respondents strongly opposed the limiting of family size.[18] An even lower percentage of disapproval was reported by Freedman and his associates from a nationwide United States sample.[19] Only 5 percent of the wives interviewed expressed unqualified disapproval of birth control practices. With the Catholic respondents eliminated the proportion dropped to 1 percent. Although differences in the wording of questions, in the meaning of "birth control," and in the nature of the respondent populations preclude exact comparisons, the general implication is that Southern Appalachian Region respondents held attitudes more similar to the Johannesburg and Puerto Rican populations than to the residents of the entire United States. Perhaps the higher percentage who disapproved of birth control practices is one explanation of the fertility rates in some areas of the region that remain above the national average.

[16] Morrison, "Indian Workers' Attitudes," 238.
[17] Edward Higgins, "Some Fertility Attitudes among White Women in Johannesburg," *Population Studies*, XVI (July 1962), 70-78.
[18] Paul K. Hatt, *Backgrounds of Human Fertility in Puerto Rico* (Princeton: Princeton University Press, 1952), 79.
[19] Freedman, Whelpton, and Campbell, *Family Planning, Sterility, and Population Growth*, 155.

5. Personal and Social Characteristics and Attitudes

The preceding chapter demonstrated that fertility change as measured by arranging counties according to 1950–1960 patterns of fertility change was meaningfully associated with differential opinions about fertility. From this finding it seems reasonable to assume that the association is one of fertility change and change in attitude and value structure.

The next point to be considered is whether there are other factors that will explain the relationship between the patterns of fertility change and the attitudinal complex associated with fertility. Especially, can the relationship be explained by personal and social characteristics of the respondents? If this is true, additional dimensions than were previously discussed are involved in the relationship. From the numerous variables that could be investigated this chapter concentrates on six—socioeconomic status, education, age, sex, parents' family size, and religious fundamentalism among Protestants. The choice of these variables was guided by prior research. Personal and social status variables are viewed from a general perspective as setting broad limits on fertility attitudes and behaviors. In other words, they are conditions within which and to which the individual reacts.[1]

The relationship between socioeconomic status and fertility is one of the most discussed correlations in research. Although the details sometimes differ according to the index used, the general conclusion has been much the same—an inverse relationship between socioeconomic status and fertility.[2] Some recent evidence suggests a weakening of this long-standing relationship. At the upper status and education levels the desired and completed family size may be higher than at middle status levels.

Socioeconomic status includes elements of both economic well-being and social prestige. While factors such as income, occupation, and education are highly correlated with socio-economic status, none by itself provides an inclusive measure. In the effort to bridge this inadequacy a composite index containing measures of several social and economic components was constructed from the Southern Appalachian Region survey data. The components of the index were household income, household equipment, the individual's own perception of his social class identification, occupation of the household head, and education of the household head. Individual scores were obtained by adding the weighted scores of the separate indicators. The respondents then were divided into four groups, ranging from lower to ·upper status, on the basis of the distribution of the scores.[3]

Education, in addition to being included in the index of socioeconomic status, was investigated separately. One reason for this was an interest in seeing if different relationships appeared for education than for socioeconomic status. Sec-

[1] Charles F. Westoff, Robert G. Potter, Jr., Philip C. Sagi, and Elliot G. Mishler, *Family Growth in Metropolitan America* (Princeton: Princeton University Press, 1961), 165-66.

[2] Edgar Sydenstricker and Frank W. Notestein, "Differential Fertility According to Social Class," *Journal of the American Statistical Association*, XXV, (March 1930), 9-32; Charles F. Westoff, "Differential Fertility in the United States: 1900 to 1952," *American Sociological Review*, XIX (Oct. 1954), 549-61; Sir Arthur Newsholme and T. H. C. Stevenson, "The Decline in Human Fertility in the United Kingdom and Other Countries as Shown by Corrected Birth Rates," *Journal of the Royal Statistical Association*, LXIX (March 1906), 34-87; Samuel A. Stouffer, "Fertility and Families on Relief," *Journal of the American Statistical Association*, XXIX (Sept. 1934), 128-51; Frank W. Notestein, "Class Differences in Fertility," *The Annals of the American Academy of Political and Social Sciences*, CLXXXVIII (Nov. 1936), 26-36; Robert M. Dinkel, "Occupation and Fertility in the United States," *American Sociological Review*, XVII (April 1952), 179-83; William F. Ogburn, "Birth Rates and Social Classes," *Social Forces*, VIII (Sept. 1929), 1-10; United Nations, *Sex and Age of International Migrants: Statistics for 1918-47*, ST/SOA/Series A/11, *Population Studies* (New York, 1953).

[3] For a detailed discussion of the socioeconomic status index, see Ralph E. Lamar, III, "Fundamentalism and Selected Factors in the Southern Appalachian Region," (unpublished Master's thesis, Dept. of Sociology, University of Kentucky, 1962), 26-27. The 1,412 individuals in this sample were divided into status categories as follows: lower–189; lower middle–365; upper middle–323; upper–173; unknown–362.

ondly, this item focuses on the education of the respondents, whereas the item included in the socioeconomic status index was based on the education of the household head.

Another social status variable included in the investigation was age. The study of response differentiation on the basis of age is one way to compensate for the lack of a time dimension in the study. This assumes that although thoughts about fertility may undergo some change over time, many basic attitudes and values remain relatively stable. These relatively stable elements reflect the socialization of the individual, which, for some survey respondents, extends from the latter part of the nineteenth century.

Parental family size is also a measure of the differential socialization of the individual. Those who grew up in large families, it was reasoned, were exposed to a type of familial structure that often may have served as a normative base for their own families. Thus, although the sizes of families have changed over the years, some congruence between broad categories of parental and sibling fertility attitudes and family size would be expected. Several studies support this general relationship.[4]

There were several reasons for including the sex of the respondent as a variable to be investigated. One was the overrepresentation of women in the Southern Appalachian Region survey. Another involves the emphasis in the patriarchal family system on the wife's role as essentially that of a mother and housekeeper. While the wife is primarily involved in the childrearing routines, the father is less exposed to the immediate concerns of the children. However, the patriarchal family system is changing, even in the Appalachians, as the greater participation of married women in the

[4] Alain Girard and Louis Henry, "Les Attitudes et la Conjoncture Démographique: Natalité Structure Familiale et Limites de la Vie Active," *Population*, XI (Jan.-March 1956), 105-15; John F. Kantner and Robert Potter, Jr., "Relationship of Family Size in Two Successive Generations," *Milbank Memorial Fund Quarterly*, XXXII (July 1954), 294-311; Jerzy Berent, "Relationship between Family Sizes of Two Successive Generations," *Milbank Memorial Fund Quarterly*, XXXI (Jan. 1953), 39-50; Marcel Bresard, "Mobilité Sociale et Dimension de la Famille," *Population*, V (July-Sept. 1950), 556-58; Westoff, Potter, Sagi, and Mishler, *Family Growth*, 287-97.

labor force would indicate. In view of these factors and the importance they hold for fertility the separate investigation of male and female response patterns seems advisable.

The influence of religion on fertility patterns has been noted in much research.[5] The general theoretical relationship between religion and fertility attitudes and behavior is well known: Catholics tend to have high fertility, Jews are at the other extreme, and Protestants occupy an intermediate position. There is, however, a paucity of research on differences in fertility among various Protestant denominations. In general it is agreed that Catholicism tends to retard the decline in fertility.[6] The Catholic Church prohibits its members from using many methods of birth control except the rhythm method, which is less efficient than some others. An analysis of Protestant-Catholic fertility differences in the Southern Appalachian Region, however, is of minimal importance, since only 2.8 percent of survey respondents identified the Roman Catholic Church as their preference. Thus, to test the importance of religious-based issues in differentiating fertility responses some means must be found to measure the differences in religious orientations among Protestants.

One simple way to classify Protestant respondents is by denominational preference, but this leaves much to be desired, since with Protestants fertility is primarily a personal

[5] Samuel A. Stouffer, "Trends in Fertility of Catholics and Non-Catholics," *American Journal of Sociology*, XLI (Sept. 1935), 143-66; Abram J. Jaffe, "Religious Differentials in the New Reproduction Rate," *Journal of the American Statistical Association*, XXXIV (June 1939), 335-42; Dudley Kirk, "Recent Trends of Catholic Fertility in the United States" in *Current Research in Human Fertility* (New York: Milbank Memorial Fund, 1955), 93-105; U.S. Bureau of the Census, *Statistical Abstract of the United States, 1958* (Washington, 1958), Table 40; Douglas G. Marshall, "The Decline in Farm Family Fertility and Its Relationship to Nationality and Religious Background," *Rural Sociology*, XV (March 1950), 42-59; Robert Gutman and Irving Bender, "Some Sources of Variation in the Family Size of College Graduates," *Milbank Memorial Fund Quarterly*, XXXV (July 1957), 287-301; Gerhard Lenski, *The Religious Factor: A Sociological Study of Religion's Impact on Politics, Economics, and Family Life* (Garden City, N. Y.: Doubleday, 1961); Ronald Freedman, Pascal K. Whelpton, and John W. Smit, "Socio-Economic Factors in Religious Differentials in Fertility," *American Sociological Review*, XXVII (Aug. 1961), 608-14.

[6] Petersen, *Population* (New York: Macmillan, 1961), 225.

rather than a denominational issue. Other fertility studies have used church attendance as a measure of "religiousness."[7] This is a questionable practice in the Southern Appalachians where, for various reasons, church attendance is not always emphasized as much as in other areas. Westoff and his associates constructed a scale of religious orientation based on responses to items in which the individual chose between religious and nonreligious themes.[8] They found that Protestant religious orientation showed little association with fertility questions.

The people of the Southern Appalachians traditionally have been characterized as having fundamentalist religious beliefs. Although this popular image may have been exaggerated, recent studies have found that it is still an important aspect of the attitude and value structure of many Appalachian residents.[9] Thus, it was deduced that if any dimension of Protestant religious orientation was significantly related to fertility attitudes, it would be the dimension of fundamentalism.

The reasoning is that the very fundamentalist individual, who interprets the Bible literally and believes that dancing and drinking are secular trends that are "always wrong," views family planning as another secular trend. Family planning is thus assumed to fall under the same condemnation as other secular activities.[10] Theoretically, then, very fundamentalist

[7] Westoff, Potter, Sagi, and Mishler, *Family Growth*, 194-211; Ronald Freedman and Pascal K. Whelpton, "Fertility Planning and Fertility Rates by Religious Interest and Denominations," *Milbank Memorial Fund Quarterly*, XXVIII (July 1950), 294-343; Ronald Freedman, Pascal K. Whelpton, and Arthur A. Campbell, *Family Planning, Sterility, and Population Growth* (New York: McGraw-Hill, 1959), 281-83.

[8] Westoff, Potter, Sagi, and Mishler, *Family Growth*, 195, 379-82.

[9] Thomas R. Ford, "The Passing of Provincialism," *SAR*, 9-34; "Status, Residence, and Fundamentalistic Religious Beliefs in the Southern Appalachians," *Social Forces*, XXXIX (Oct. 1960), 41-49; Gordon F. De Jong and Thomas R. Ford, "Religious Fundamentalism and Denominational Preference in the Southern Appalachian Region," *Journal for the Scientific Study of Religion*, V (Fall 1965), 24-33.

[10] Viewing birth control as a secular trend is not a new idea. See, for example, Frederick L. Hoffman, "The Decline in the Birth Rate," *North American Review*, CLXXXVIX (May 1909), 677-87; and Frederick S. Crum, "The Decadence of the Native American Stock," *Journal of the American Statistical Association*, XIV (Sept. 1914), 215-22.

religious orientations would be associated with higher fertility, and nonfundamentalist orientations would be associated with lower fertility.

To provide a measure of fundamentalist orientation the responses to a number of relevant belief and attitude questions were analyzed for scalability.[11] Dichotomized responses to six items on a questionnaire yielded a Guttman scale with a coefficient of reproducibility of .92. The scale includes six items: attitude toward gambling; attitude toward drinking; view of religious doctrine (ultimate reliance upon Biblical authority); view on the importance of "calling" for the ministry; attitude toward card playing; and view on the coming of the end of the world. Individual scale scores were grouped into four categories on the basis of common response patterns.

In this analysis the focus is not on the relationships among personal and social characteristics and opinion responses.[12] Rather, the main issue is the manner in which the introduction of personal and social characteristics as control variables affects the previously observed relationships among the opinion responses and the county fertility types.

The introduction of control variables modifies the interpretative model that was used in the preceding chapter. In the first model the relationship was a direct one between two factors—attitudes and the patterns of county fertility change. Of course, this model did not indicate the direction of causal influence—whether changes in attitudes produced fertility changes or fertility changes produced changes in attitudes. The assumption was that attitudes produced fertility changes. In this chapter the interpretative model focuses on an indirect relationship between attitudes and fertility. The relationship is indirect in the sense that various personal and social status categories act as intervening variables. Again, a causal relationship cannot be determined; however, it is possible to give some indication of the influence of personal and social characteristics.

[11] Lamar, "Fundamentalism," 28-30, 88-97.
[12] For this analysis see Gordon F. De Jong, "Religious Fundamentalism, Socio-Economic Status, and Fertility Attitudes in the Southern Appalachians," *Demography*, II (1965), 540-48.

Ideally, an analysis of this type would employ a multivariate statistical model, such as multiple correlation. Unfortunately, the data do not meet the assumptions of a multiple correlation model. Some of the data, for instance, do not form interval scales. Frequently the distributions approximate a J-curve rather than the normal curve. Consequently, Chi-squares for zero-order and first-order cross-classifications will be used to indicate the nature of the relationship between fertility opinion responses and county fertility type for each control variable category.

An example of how the model works may be useful in understanding the analysis. A statistically significant difference was found to exist between each of the six opinion statements about fertility and county fertility change groupings (see chapter four). The same relationships will now be tested with controls of certain personal and social characteristics of the respondents added. For example, with socioeconomic status as a control variable three possible interpretations could arise from the use of this model.

First, the originally observed significant relationship between opinion responses and county fertility type may persist, even when the control variable, in this case socioeconomic status, is introduced. This would support the original conclusion that opinions are related to fertility change, since the controlling for socioeconomic differences does not alter the relationship.

Second, the statistically significant relationship between opinion responses and county fertility type may disappear when the control variable of socioeconomic status is introduced. This does not necessarily establish that the real relationship is between socioeconomic status and county fertility change patterns. Further investigation would be needed to show whether this relationship did, in fact, exist. However, it would indicate that the originally observed relationship is explained by some other variable. And, apparently, the explanatory variable is the one used as a statistical control, such as socioeconomic status.

Third, and more complex, the statistically significant relationship between opinion responses and county fertility type may consistently disappear for some segments of the control, for example, lower socioeconomic status, and consistently remain for other segments of the control, for instance, upper socioeconomic status. Consistent disappearance of the original relationship for segments of the control variable would be suggestive of an additional or alternative explanatory factor, while for other segments of the control variable the original conclusion would be substantiated.

The major findings can be summarized briefly. When the responses to all six opinion statements as a unit were considered, the relationship with county fertility change patterns persisted in a majority of the breakdowns, even when the distributions were controlled for personal and social characteristics (Table 29). Nearly two-thirds of the relationships remained significant at the .05 level or beyond, and some of the other distributions were close to statistical significance. From an overall view the findings tend to substantiate the original conclusion that a significant relationship exists between attitudinal patterns and fertility change.

However, there were three notable and undoubtedly related exceptions to the general conclusion. The relationship between opinion response patterns and county fertility type disappeared for all but one opinion among the lower socioeconomic status group. On this one item—ideal age at marriage for a man—the difference was just significant at the .05 level (Table 29). A similar exception was noted when the relationship was controlled by education. Among respondents with six years of schooling or less there was only one statistically significant difference—between county fertility types and ideal number of children for a well-off couple. The third exception was for respondents who had very fundamentalist religious beliefs. Again, for only one opinion—ideal number of children for the not well-off couple—was there a statistically significant difference at the .05 level. In each case the statistically significant relationship appeared for the answers to different opinion questions, which suggests that the variation was not systematic. The important point, however, is that the previously observed significant relationship between opinion responses and county fertility change patterns con-

TABLE 29

Relationship between Fertility Opinion Responses and County Fertility Type Controlled by Specific Personal and Social Characteristics for White Respondents in the Southern Appalachian Region, 1958

Personal and Social Characteristics	LEVEL OF SIGNIFICANCE OF RELATIONSHIP					
	Ideal Number of Children			Ideal Age at Marriage		Birth Control Practices
	Average Couple	Well-off Couple	Not Well-off Couple	Woman	Man	
Socioeconomic status						
Lower	N.S.	N.S.	N.S.	N.S.	.05	N.S.
Lower Middle	N.S.	N.S.	.05	N.S.	.001	N.S.
Upper Middle	.02	.01	.01	.001	.01	N.S.
Upper	.001	.001	N.S.	.001	.001	N.S.
Education						
6 years or less	N.S.	.05	N.S.	N.S.	N.S.	N.S.
7 and 8 years	N.S.	N.S.	.02	.02	N.S.	.05
9-11 years	N.S.	N.S.	.001	N.S.	.05	N.S.
12 years	.001	N.S.	.05	N.S.	.05	N.S.
13 years or more	.01	.05	.01	.001	.001	N.S.
Religious fundamentalism						
Not very fundamental	.01	N.S.	.01	.001	.001	N.S.
Moderately fundamental	N.S.	.01	N.S.	N.S.	.05	N.S.
Essentially fundamental	.001	N.S.	.001	.001	.05	.01
Very fundamental	N.S.	N.S.	.05	N.S.	N.S.	N.S.

TABLE 29 (continued)

<table>
<tr><th rowspan="2">Personal and Social Characteristics</th><th colspan="6">LEVEL OF SIGNIFICANCE OF RELATIONSHIP</th></tr>
<tr><th>Ideal Number of Children — Average Couple</th><th>Well-off Couple</th><th>Not Well-off Couple</th><th>Ideal Age at Marriage — Woman</th><th>Man</th><th>Birth Control Practices</th></tr>
<tr><td>Age</td><td></td><td></td><td></td><td></td><td></td><td></td></tr>
<tr><td>Under 30 years</td><td>.001</td><td>.01</td><td>.01</td><td>.05</td><td>N.S.</td><td>N.S.</td></tr>
<tr><td>30-44 years</td><td>.05</td><td>N.S.</td><td>N.S.</td><td>.001</td><td>.001</td><td>.05</td></tr>
<tr><td>45-64 years</td><td>.001</td><td>.01</td><td>.001</td><td>.001</td><td>.001</td><td>.01</td></tr>
<tr><td>65 years and over</td><td>N.S.</td><td>.02</td><td>.02</td><td>.001</td><td>N.S.</td><td>.001</td></tr>
<tr><td>Parental Family Size</td><td></td><td></td><td></td><td></td><td></td><td></td></tr>
<tr><td>1-4 children</td><td>.001</td><td>N.S.</td><td>.001</td><td>.001</td><td>.001</td><td>.001</td></tr>
<tr><td>5-7 children</td><td>.02</td><td>.001</td><td>.001</td><td>.001</td><td>.02</td><td>.01</td></tr>
<tr><td>8 children or more</td><td>.01</td><td>N.S.</td><td>.02</td><td>.001</td><td>.001</td><td>.05</td></tr>
<tr><td>Sex</td><td></td><td></td><td></td><td></td><td></td><td></td></tr>
<tr><td>Male</td><td>.001</td><td>.001</td><td>.001</td><td>.001</td><td>.01</td><td>.001</td></tr>
<tr><td>Female</td><td>.001</td><td>.05</td><td>.001</td><td>.001</td><td>.001</td><td>.001</td></tr>
</table>

N.S. means "not significant."

sistently disappeared when the controls of these three personal and social characteristics were introduced.

The relationship between opinion responses and county fertility change patterns also tended to disappear for the lower-middle socioeconomic status group, those with nine to eleven years of schooling, and those with moderately fundamental religious beliefs. However, within these categories some of the distributions were highly significant statistically. This finding casts some doubt on the nature and consistency of these segments of the control variables.

The consistent absence of significant relationships between fertility change patterns and opinion responses for certain groupings of respondents is an important finding. Of course, the overall pattern remains: fertility change is, in part, related to attitude and value differences. Respondents in predominantly rural areas designated stronger attitudes supporting higher fertility than did respondents in urban areas. And, as recent research has indicated, attitudes are becoming increasingly reliable as predictors of actual fertility behavior.[13]

The findings suggest that some factors are operative in the experiences of the respondents with lower socioeconomic status, with six years of formal education or less, and with very fundamental religious beliefs that produce similar response patterns regardless of whether the individual lived in predominantly rural, high fertility areas or predominantly urban, low fertility areas. In other words, the mountaineer and his city cousin with the same characteristics may not differ greatly in their attitudes about fertility and family size.

An important factor here may be internal migration within Appalachia. Urban areas have received a sizable influx of rural migrants during the past twenty years. It is plausible that some of the respondents in the predominantly urban, low fertility areas were reared in rural Appalachia. It would not be surprising, then, if many of the basic values were similar to those of respondents who still live in rural Appalachia. Although it is in a different context, Goldberg's research supports this conclusion in demonstrating that fertility is

[13] Charles F. Westoff, Robert G. Potter, Jr., and Philip C. Sagi, *The Third Child* (Princeton: Princeton University Press, 1963).

higher for urban residents who were reared in rural areas than for urban residents who were reared in the city.[14]

The study by Lee Rainwater, *And the Poor Get Children,* provides perhaps the most thorough documentation of the attitudes of respondents with low education and low socioeconomic status toward sex and family planning.[15] The study is particularly applicable, because approximately one-half of his one hundred interviews were with working-class respondents living in Cincinnati. The majority of these were migrants with "Southern rural" backgrounds. Rainwater found that his respondents had attitudes and values characterized by myths and inadequate information about sex and fertility, which tended to impede family planning and to enhance relatively high fertility. Based on the findings here, one could hypothesize that Rainwater might have found much the same conditions in an extension of his study to rural Appalachian respondents.

A newly analyzed element that affects fertility is Protestant religious fundamentalism. The data indicate that respondents characterized as very fundamental had much the same attitudes about fertility regardless of whether they lived in predominantly rural, high fertility areas or predominantly urban, low fertility areas. It can be argued that in reference to fertility issues religious fundamentalism actually refers to much the same factor as does low socioeconomic status. However, further analysis has indicated that fundamentalism, particularly high fundamentalism, is important even when socioeconomic status is taken into account.[16]

The influence of fundamentalism on fertility issues seems to stem from the consequences of this system of religious beliefs. A salient feature of fundamentalism is the literal interpretation of the Bible, and perhaps the best known Biblical reference to fertility is the command to "be fruitful,

[14] David Goldberg, "The Fertility of Two Generation Urbanites," *Population Studies,* XV (Nov. 1961), 161-73; "Another Look at the Indianapolis Fertility Data," *Milbank Memorial Fund Quarterly,* XXVIII (Jan. 1960), 23-36.

[15] Lee Rainwater, *And the Poor Get Children* (Chicago: Quadrangle Books, 1960).

[16] De Jong, "Religious Fundamentalism and Fertility Attitudes."

6. Toward Theory and Application

Many of Appalachia's population trends and characteristics are conspicuous in their divergence from national trends. In 1960 a majority of the people still lived in rural areas. Very few Negroes lived in the region. The region contained proportionally more youths but fewer adults, particularly young adults. The level of educational attainment averaged about two years less than the national level. There were fewer males employed in white-collar occupations. Also, the median family income was only about two-thirds that of the nation. Appalachian fertility patterns, however, began to resemble those of the nation.

Several conclusions can be drawn from the analysis. Between 1930 and 1960 there was a marked decline in fertility for the white population of the Southern Appalachian Region. The ecology of the decline indicated that the lowest fertility rates were initially found in metropolitan counties and other counties located in the valley areas. By 1960 the lowest rates had spread to some peripheral counties, and the high fertility rates prevailed primarily in the most rural, upland areas of the region.

The analysis of the effects of migration on fertility change through the alteration of the number of people in the child-bearing age groups indicated that migration was undeniably significant but only a partial explanation for fertility decline. Another partial explanation was the rural-urban differential in fertility. The 1950-1960 rural to urban population shifts generally supported the contention that changes in residential patterns are related to fertility decline.

Insights into the attitude and value structure related to fertility and family size were provided by analyzing survey data on ideal family size, ideal age at marriage, and opinions about birth control practices. The data provided consistent evidence that fertility change was related to these manifestations of the respondents' attitudes and values. The associations generally persisted even when personal and social characteristics were introduced as control variables. However, for respondents with lower socioeconomic status, six years or less of formal education, or very fundamental religious beliefs, fertility decline was not significantly associated with attitudes about fertility.

In sum, fertility decline in the Southern Appalachian Region was associated with the demographic variable of migration (through the alteration of the number of women in the childbearing age groups) and with the sociological variables of residence and attitudes and values.

SOME IMPLICATIONS FOR THEORY AND RESEARCH

An issue of considerable interest to social demographers is the process of family limitation—a critical link in explaining demographic transition. Why does a husband and/or wife decide to limit family size? The research literature identifies numerous correlated variables, such as religion and age at marriage, but the key motivational factors still are uncertain. One approach is to consider family size within the broader context of rationally established individual and family goals. The number of children is then viewed in relation to other economically and socially defined items that the individual or family desires. In the decision-making process attitudes about fertility and family size may be determined in part by the perceived economic costs of children.

While the present research did not test this thesis, some tangential evidence is available. Appalachian residents were asked what they considered an ideal family size for an average couple, an economically well-off couple, and an economically not well-off couple. For all three questions respondents living in predominantly urban, low fertility areas expressed a lower median family size ideal than did respondents living in predominantly rural, high fertility areas. However, when the medians for well-off and not well-off couples were compared to the median for an average couple, the rural, high fertility area respondents reported a smaller increase and a larger decrease for well-off and not well-off economic statuses, respectively, than did urban, low fertility area respondents. It may be that the respondents living in predominantly rural, high fertility areas are more sensitive to the economic costs of children. If this is true the attempts to get actual family size to correspond to desired family size would seem to be a striking problem for many rural Appalachian families who would not be considered well-off economically. The data provide a bit of evidence on what may be a critical variable in the process of family limitation.

The significance of religious fundamentalism as a factor in differential fertility suggests a largely unexplored area of research. The logic of the relationship would seem to stem from the consequences of fundamentalist religious beliefs. A basic tenet of fundamentalism is the literal interpretation of the Bible. Perhaps the best known Biblical references to fertility emphasize the command to "be fruitful and multiply." Also, the fundamentalist is likely to act on the assumption that life proceeds according to the will of God and to believe that the attempt to regulate conception interferes with God's plan. This line of reasoning is concerned primarily with the ideological dimension of a fundamentalist religious orientation and leaves untouched the possible influences of the experiential (emotional) and ritualistic (prayer, attendance of "preaching" services) aspects of religious fundamentalism. All these factors would need to be considered in evaluating the source and character of the religious fundamentalism factor.

The finding that low socioeconomic status, low education, and high fundamentalism appear to statistically explain the relationship between fertility decline and the measured attitude structure can be interpreted in several ways. First, the disappearance of the relationships may have been the result of insensitive measuring instruments. The fertility change data were based on county units, not on the particular individuals who were investigated. Of course, the fertility of these individuals was included in the total county fertility rates. Nevertheless, one still must deal with the fact that the absence of a significant relationship among county fertility change patterns and attitudes was noted consistently for only these three groups and not for any of the other control groups.

A second possibility is that these three groupings of respondents had not developed, at least on a conscious level, pervasive attitudes or values about fertility and family size. Although most responded to the opinion questions about fertility, their responses showed an inconsistent association with fertility change. This perhaps indicates a case in which the attitudes made little measurable difference. Though not directly analogous, this situation resembles somewhat the one that Yaukey found in studying Lebanese couples. When asked about family size, almost two-thirds of the uneducated village women simply responded with "as God wills" or "as many as possible."[1]

There is another possible explanation of the lack of association between county fertility change patterns and attitudes for respondents with low socioeconomic status, for respondents with six years of formal education or less, and for respondents with very fundamentalist religious beliefs. Respondents with these characteristics apparently held much the same opinions about fertility and family size regardless of where they lived. This could mean that these respondents, far from having no attitudes about fertility, had very rigid attitudes on the subject—attitudes that were not significantly affected by the prevailing attitude and value structures of the residents of the counties in which they lived. As a consequence of these attitudes, their opinion responses were not significantly associated with county fertility change patterns. It could be reasoned further that this rigidity was determined to a great extent by early socialization, which apparently differed in some ways from the socialization of persons of other statuses and religious groups. The fertility attitudes of individuals other than those of lower socioeconomic status, low education, and very fundamental religious beliefs were

[1] David Yaukey, *Fertility Differences in a Modernizing Country* (Princeton: Princeton University Press, 1961), 72-76.

perhaps more amenable to change, as indicated by the observed association between attitudes and county fertility change patterns.

A different type of consideration is the possible relationship between migration and fertility attitudes and values. Are high fertility attitudes of Appalachian residents affected by the back-and-forth migration to non-Appalachian urban areas? Although the major interactional patterns during this migration may stay within the extended family, there is at least a minimal contact with different attitude and value complexes. The present research has shown that the place of residence makes little difference in fertility attitudes of respondents with certain characteristics, but it has not explained why. Is it a lack of contact with the "greater society," not only by migrants but also by the residents of urban areas with whom the migrants associate?[2] These issues appear worthy of further research, which could have both demographic and sociological significance.

SOME IMPLICATIONS FOR APPALACHIAN DEVELOPMENT

From a broad perspective there is a dual approach to the strategy of Appalachian development. One focuses on the frequently emphasized problems of physical resources and industrialization (area development), while the second focuses on human resources (human development).[3] Obviously, one approach must be considered in relation to the other. Nevertheless, the two approaches have some unique features that can be considered separately, at least analytically. Since this study investigated aspects of population change, its implications for Appalachian development rather naturally fall into the category of factors influencing human resources.

[2] James S. Brown, Harry K. Schwarzweller, and Joseph J. Mangalam, "Kentucky Mountain Migration and the Stem-family: An American Variation on a Theme by Le Play," *Rural Sociology*, XXVIII (March 1963), 48-69; Harry K. Schwarzweller and James S. Brown, "Education as a Cultural Bridge between Eastern Kentucky and the Great Society," *Rural Sociology*, XXVII (Dec. 1962), 357-73.

[3] For a more detailed consideration of these two approaches, see Rupert B. Vance, "The Region's Future: A National Challenge," in *SAR*, 289-99.

High fertility is frequently linked to poverty. In the United States, and particularly in the Appalachians, a disproportionate number of the very poor families continue to have a large number of children, and thus poverty tends to be self-perpetuating. The imbalance of population and economy is not unique to the Southern Appalachian Region. In addition to other areas in the United States today, there are numerous historical examples from the days of the children of Israel, to the industrialization period in Europe, to the Irish potato famine. Although each example is in some way different, a common thread in them all is a similar corrective strategy—migration to other areas that would afford a better opportunity for making a living. So the children of Israel moved their flocks to new grazing lands; the displaced workers of the industrial revolution migrated to central Russia, the new world, and other colonial lands; and the hungry Irishmen crossed the Atlantic to the United States.

The Southern Appalachians could be added to this list of examples. While private and government programs have had a corrective influence in some local areas, the people of Appalachia, especially the youth, are providing an answer by migrating from the region. This does not mean that efforts for area development are futile. Rather, it calls attention to one corrective measure that is not only currently in process but has been taking place for more than two decades. Between 1950 and 1960 the region's population declined for the first time since census data have been available. The evidence would seem to indicate that a point of equilibrium may soon be reached in the valley area of Appalachia where the population increased slightly during the 1950–1960 period, although even here more people have migrated out than have migrated into the valley.

The decisions of people to move from the region are not prompted by a concern for area development. Rather, they are decisions made by individuals as members of family units, reached within the structural conditions of economic deprivation, hastened by peer-group pressures, and facilitated by the extended family system whose members frequently reside in employment centers outside the region. But while the decisions may have been made within the context of a small group, their consequences extend far beyond these bound-aries. Some of these consequences are undoubtedly dysfunc-tional both to the individuals and the areas, but other conse-quences are certainly functional.

Out-migration has not been the only response to Appala-chia's population-economy imbalance. Changes in the at-titude and value structure also affect population size. As with migration, certain areas within the region are affected more than others, and the fertility attitudes and values of rural residents are generally slower to change than those of urban dwellers. To the extent that a decline in the birth rate is functional to the development efforts, very low educa-tion and socioeconomic status and very fundamental religious beliefs may impede change and perpetuate high fertility.

The success of the future development efforts in the South-ern Appalachian Region depends not only on the traditionally emphasized programs of area development but also on precedent shattering designs in human development. Indeed, it seems quite unlikely that the entire range of private and government programs in area development will have as much immediate effect on the population-economy imbalance as will continued out-migration and changes toward a smaller family size. One explanation for the spread of these trends is the strong desire of most Appalachian residents, and par-ticularly the youth, to enjoy the goods and services of the affluent society. Building on this motivational base is a major task of development policy. In areas in which the prospects of immediate economic opportunities are poor, planners should recognize a fact that the young people of these areas have known for years—that to be participants in the affluent society they have to leave the Appalachians. Efforts to augment rather than impede these decisions to leave would be unique, especially if the efforts included thorough educational and occupational preparation for automation and urbanization. These efforts obviously eclipse the traditional social and political norms of the role of state-oriented educational sys-tems. Nevertheless, such efforts could have significant conse-quences for individual and for area development, whether in or out of the Southern Appalachians.

Appendix A

FERTILITY DATA FOR SOUTHERN APPALACHIAN REGION COUNTIES, 1930–1960

TABLE 1

Crude Birth Rates for the White Population of the United States, the Southern Appalachian Region, and Southern Appalachian Region Counties, 1960, 1950, 1940, and 1930[a]

Area	1960	1950	1940	1930
United States	22.7	23.0	18.6	20.6
Southern Appalachian Region, Total	23.0	28.0	30.2	30.1
Alabama				
Area 2				
Blount	20.6	24.9	29.1	36.2
Cullman	21.2	26.1	29.5	32.2
DeKalb	19.8	25.4	27.3	37.8
Jackson	25.7	30.3	33.0	35.1
Marshall	25.9	29.9	24.9	29.6
Georgia				
Metropolitan Area A				
Walker	20.7	17.0	28.7	29.5
Area 1				
Bartow	25.1	29.7	29.6	21.4
Catoosa	23.1	26.0	19.5	22.6
Chattooga	24.6	28.3	32.2	32.1
Dade	25.2	32.2	32.8	39.6
Floyd	21.6	23.8	28.1	27.3
Gordon	22.9	24.3	30.0	30.4
Murray	18.8	29.4	30.2	32.5
Polk	23.5	26.2	28.0	27.8
Whitfield	25.3	28.7	29.4	35.8

[a] Based on average annual births for the periods 1929-1931, 1939-1941, 1949-1951, and 1959-1960, adjusted for underregistration.

TABLE 1 *(continued)*

Area	1960	1950	1940	1930
Area 2				
Dawson	20.8	25.7	35.6	35.4
Fannin	17.7	27.0	30.7	38.6
Gilmer	16.3	28.5	35.0	36.3
Habersham	23.6	25.9	28.5	29.0
Lumpkin	23.6	24.9	26.9	28.8
Pickens	28.7	32.6	27.4	28.3
Rabun	22.2	27.0	39.0	27.7
Towns	16.4	23.6	27.4	35.1
Union	17.9	25.4	32.1	33.4
White	24.6	29.2	31.2	35.5
Kentucky				
Metropolitan Area C				
Boyd	22.0	26.9	25.8	26.5
Area 8				
Carter	25.0	30.0	32.2	30.7
Clay	32.1	35.0	38.9	39.7
Elliott	23.5	32.8	35.3	47.7
Estill	22.5	25.4	28.7	31.1
Greenup	24.2	28.8	27.3	26.5
Jackson	23.6	30.5	30.4	31.8
Laurel	24.9	29.4	27.8	25.2
Lawrence	23.1	26.6	27.5	28.1
Lee	26.7	33.7	26.2	29.9
Lewis	26.8	33.5	30.0	30.9
Magoffin	27.3	40.3	40.5	39.8
Menifee	24.3	30.3	32.3	31.5
Morgan	25.9	29.3	31.8	37.6
Owsley	24.4	33.8	40.9	46.9
Powell	26.4	30.6	28.1	31.3
Rowan	22.7	27.1	33.5	34.7
Wolfe	30.6	30.9	34.7	26.7
Area 9				
Bell	25.9	34.5	35.2	28.1
Breathitt	29.3	31.2	36.8	37.0
Floyd	27.7	36.7	35.1	33.7
Harlan	27.4	35.0	35.8	37.4
Johnson	22.5	31.0	33.1	31.8
Knott	23.4	33.8	37.8	41.8
Knox	24.5	27.9	31.9	32.8
Leslie	43.1	40.2	37.1	37.5
Letcher	27.6	36.4	36.9	33.4
McCreary	27.5	31.5	38.9	26.1

TABLE 1 *(continued)*

Area	1960	1950	1940	1930
Martin	28.6	37.0	36.4	32.7
Perry	31.1	39.8	37.4	45.8
Pike	26.4	36.7	36.9	38.3
Whitley	21.6	26.4	31.5	37.8
North Carolina				
Metropolitan Area A				
Buncombe	20.4	22.3	23.7	22.9
Area 1				
Alleghany	19.6	21.5	23.5	26.6
Ashe	22.8	27.9	29.1	33.4
Avery	23.4	27.8	35.9	38.1
Cherokee	19.0	26.8	35.2	29.4
Clay	23.9	25.5	35.5	38.5
Graham	24.2	30.6	39.2	31.8
Haywood	23.5	26.5	30.2	32.2
Henderson	20.4	26.6	26.8	27.2
Jackson	20.3	26.3	28.5	29.9
Macon	18.9	24.5	30.8	33.1
Madison	18.2	22.4	28.9	31.6
Mitchell	22.5	27.0	30.0	34.8
Swain	22.3	25.6	36.9	29.2
Transylvania	24.7	32.9	35.4	34.8
Watauga	21.2	26.6	27.8	31.2
Yancey	20.2	26.0	29.1	28.2
Area 2				
Alexander	22.3	27.3	31.2	32.7
Burke	20.9	25.4	29.9	29.5
Caldwell	26.8	30.8	33.4	34.3
McDowell	25.0	29.9	30.0	32.7
Wilkes	23.2	27.7	32.1	36.7
Tennessee				
Metropolitan Area C				
Hamilton	23.1	25.8	27.7	17.7
Metropolitan Area D				
Anderson	24.9	31.1	28.8	31.0
Blount	21.3	27.8	32.1	29.6
Knox	22.5	24.3	24.1	18.4
Area 7				
Bledsoe	24.7	31.4	33.9	23.9
Cumberland	25.1	28.9	27.9	27.7
Fentress	27.7	32.0	44.6	38.8
Grundy	26.0	28.8	31.2	25.7
Marion	24.0	29.4	35.1	29.5

Appendix A

TABLE 1 *(continued)*

Area	1960	1950	1940	1930
Morgan	20.5	25.5	30.3	34.8
Scott	25.3	32.7	57.0	54.7
Sequatchie	19.4	24.1	30.9	27.8
Van Buren	25.6	25.9	36.8	51.3
Area 8a				
Bradley	24.7	33.5	28.1	30.1
Campbell	22.9	29.4	38.5	34.5
Loudon	21.4	25.0	27.1	28.7
McMinn	22.3	25.4	27.2	30.1
Meigs	20.5	31.0	31.7	25.5
Monroe	23.8	29.4	34.9	30.9
Polk	23.6	30.2	30.0	43.4
Rhea	24.7	27.7	32.4	22.6
Roane	23.3	28.9	29.1	32.2
Sevier	21.4	25.4	31.5	33.3
Union	21.4	29.0	55.9	50.2
Area 8b				
Carter	19.1	25.2	30.9	31.3
Claiborne	21.7	25.9	35.3	25.7
Cocke	24.3	29.7	28.9	33.4
Grainger	23.3	24.4	28.2	25.7
Greene	20.7	24.2	24.2	26.0
Hamblen	21.7	27.2	25.7	24.1
Hancock	23.7	28.0	35.2	42.6
Hawkins	22.4	27.3	30.3	33.0
Jefferson	21.3	23.5	31.2	29.0
Johnson	18.2	25.4	34.1	36.2
Sullivan	22.4	27.8	28.3	20.8
Unicoi	23.3	25.9	40.2	28.6
Washington	24.2	26.0	26.3	24.0
Virginia				
Metropolitan Area A				
Roanoke	20.5	22.9	22.7	24.5
Area 1				
Buchanan	30.8	36.5	43.6	47.1
Dickenson	25.7	33.5	37.7	39.0
Lee	19.8	28.5	31.1	33.7
Tazewell	25.7	35.1	37.7	38.2
Wise	25.2	32.0	32.0	35.1
Area 2				
Bland	16.0	23.0	26.8	25.7
Carroll	19.0	22.5	23.7	30.9

TABLE 1 *(continued)*

Area	1960	1950	1940	1930
Grayson	20.9	26.3	26.3	29.5
Russell	23.1	29.4	32.7	34.9
Scott	20.9	25.3	30.9	33.5
Smyth	22.3	24.9	29.0	34.1
Washington	22.3	27.6	29.0	28.7
Wythe	20.0	27.9	22.9	32.6
Area 3				
Alleghany	21.2	27.7	23.1	24.9
Bath	21.0	21.2	23.8	20.0
Botetourt	19.3	20.9	24.4	24.4
Craig	18.8	21.5	19.7	22.0
Floyd	18.1	20.3	25.6	26.3
Giles	19.4	30.2	30.5	33.7
Highland	18.4	19.7	31.8	28.3
Montgomery	23.3	26.0	26.3	24.9
Pulaski	20.8	27.2	28.9	28.6
Rockbridge	25.1	24.8	24.4	26.6
Area 4				
Augusta	26.8	23.1	23.0	21.3
Clarke	22.0	25.1	28.1	23.5
Frederick	18.6	24.7	23.7	26.4
Page	20.9	25.0	25.3	31.4
Rockingham	22.5	24.9	24.2	26.0
Shenandoah	18.9	21.8	21.8	24.6
Warren	21.0	27.3	26.7	26.2
West Virginia				
Metropolitan Area B				
Cabell	21.9	25.7	23.7	22.5
Wayne	21.5	25.2	28.2	28.6
Metropolitan Area C				
Kanawha	24.1	29.8	35.1	29.5
Fayette	21.0	29.2	29.9	32.9
Area 2b				
Braxton	22.7	27.3	26.0	27.0
Calhoun	19.9	23.2	29.5	30.8
Clay	27.1	36.3	32.3	32.0
Doddridge	18.8	19.9	22.7	28.4
Gilmer	21.8	20.4	25.3	27.7
Lewis	18.0	20.3	18.6	20.7
Nicholas	23.4	31.5	27.5	33.7
Ritchie	19.2	21.2	21.4	23.4
Roane	17.1	22.4	23.1	26.6

Appendix A

TABLE 1 *(continued)*

Area	1960	1950	1940	1930
Upshur	20.8	26.4	23.3	25.4
Webster	24.0	29.4	30.0	31.5
Wirt	20.1	18.7	21.6	20.5
Area 3				
Barbour	20.2	23.5	29.7	30.0
Harrison	20.9	24.1	23.4	25.7
Marion	19.5	24.5	24.5	25.2
Monongalia	21.0	24.7	23.2	28.6
Preston	23.6	26.3	26.9	29.2
Taylor	18.1	23.3	21.2	23.9
Area 4				
Boone	22.7	31.9	34.1	37.4
Logan	25.8	36.0	36.2	38.7
McDowell	26.8	38.3	44.0	39.3
Mercer	21.9	27.2	32.5	32.3
Mingo	28.2	38.6	38.0	32.4
Raleigh	22.4	29.8	38.6	40.8
Wyoming	25.1	35.2	42.6	37.7
Area 5				
Grant	25.3	28.9	34.6	29.4
Greenbrier	22.6	29.9	27.8	30.9
Hampshire	19.0	22.2	24.3	26.8
Hardy	22.6	23.5	26.0	29.7
Mineral	20.9	26.1	25.0	23.9
Monroe	17.2	22.9	24.1	21.8
Pendleton	20.5	25.5	30.5	31.8
Pocahontas	23.8	29.5	26.7	27.7
Randolph	23.9	26.8	31.4	29.5
Summers	19.4	25.0	24.1	26.3
Tucker	21.7	24.8	24.3	26.9
Area 6				
Berkeley	21.8	24.0	19.7	24.5
Jefferson	21.8	25.5	28.0	27.3
Morgan	23.3	28.7	23.5	27.5

TABLE 2

Fertility Ratios for the White Population of the United States, the Southern Appalachian Region, and Southern Appalachian Region Counties, 1960, 1950, 1940, and 1930

Area	1960	1950	1940	1930
United States	545.9	466.8	323.5	390.0
Southern Appalachian Region, Total	511.5	549.6	480.6	585.0
Alabama				
Area 2				
Blount	507.5	561.5	513.1	628.7
Cullman	559.6	557.6	488.9	640.8
DeKalb	519.4	530.8	461.7	616.5
Jackson	535.5	600.5	574.5	657.2
Marshall	542.7	527.3	463.5	596.8
Georgia				
Metropolitan Area A				
Walker	512.4	528.3	431.0	536.2
Area 1				
Bartow	490.9	537.2	453.7	538.3
Catoosa	563.8	562.8	462.3	571.2
Chattooga	512.9	512.7	443.8	558.1
Dade	633.7	660.1	560.0	651.2
Floyd	476.7	425.8	366.6	459.9
Gordon	499.7	525.3	438.2	535.5
Murray	554.7	603.0	583.7	647.5
Polk	497.1	510.4	423.1	533.0
Whitfield	536.2	503.7	407.5	509.4
Area 2				
Dawson	523.4	638.5	610.3	586.3
Fannin	485.2	612.8	603.6	714.5
Gilmer	541.8	610.8	529.3	679.1
Habersham	524.5	580.1	476.3	591.3
Lumpkin	471.4	610.1	580.3	627.8
Pickens	575.7	551.7	470.2	623.0
Rabun	541.2	678.7	512.8	620.0
Towns	445.7	588.2	549.1	645.7
Union	541.6	614.2	572.6	344.5
White	524.5	584.1	568.5	650.9
Kentucky				
Metropolitan Area C				
Boyd	537.4	497.0	406.6	516.0
Area 8				
Carter	585.6	627.2	638.2	714.1

TABLE 2 *(continued)*

Area	1960	1950	1940	1930
Clay	740.0	824.1	728.0	807.0
Elliott	658.5	713.8	727.8	748.3
Estill	549.4	599.5	524.2	680.6
Greenup	603.9	610.1	534.4	692.7
Jackson	605.7	681.5	764.1	756.3
Laurel	568.9	642.0	551.0	675.0
Lawrence	608.6	606.9	555.3	648.2
Lee	702.2	745.5	586.8	703.4
Lewis	636.1	659.5	597.2	699.8
Magoffin	698.9	777.0	733.2	738.8
Menifee	639.8	763.6	648.2	722.1
Morgan	637.3	693.8	623.4	700.3
Owsley	617.5	729.9	621.7	730.2
Powell	693.2	700.1	618.4	686.3
Rowan	469.7	573.2	586.7	717.1
Wolfe	754.2	669.9	654.8	760.1
Area 9				
Bell	568.7	678.5	554.9	649.5
Breathitt	676.2	739.3	732.5	762.0
Floyd	600.1	748.9	653.8	814.6
Harlan	554.2	675.1	576.6	746.7
Johnson	546.1	611.1	575.0	677.6
Knott	663.7	777.4	723.3	876.4
Knox	566.1	667.0	570.1	645.6
Leslie	868.9	828.6	819.2	922.2
Letcher	617.8	697.7	667.8	823.5
McCreary	632.6	750.7	678.7	788.6
Martin	759.2	843.7	722.5	827.7
Perry	662.1	750.8	668.4	814.8
Pike	595.0	717.2	643.5	805.2
Whitley	523.1	577.6	505.5	597.0
North Carolina				
Metropolitan Area A				
Buncombe	453.8	445.0	349.5	430.6
Area 1				
Alleghany	452.7	533.0	461.8	607.9
Ashe	498.2	600.4	539.3	637.9
Avery	440.2	600.6	594.3	675.3
Cherokee	497.9	639.7	546.1	621.8
Clay	537.6	639.4	543.2	662.3
Graham	534.7	662.6	614.3	742.3
Haywood	476.6	545.9	504.0	648.8
Henderson	474.1	496.6	386.0	498.2

TABLE 2 *(continued)*

Area	1960	1950	1940	1930
Jackson	400.8	588.9	553.8	666.0
Macon	475.7	610.2	567.9	628.5
Madison	419.2	518.8	533.8	654.9
Mitchell	474.8	559.5	548.2	687.2
Swain	500.4	627.6	597.1	677.0
Transylvania	488.5	567.7	500.0	566.3
Watauga	388.3	529.4	566.9	664.1
Yancey	463.2	612.3	574.2	667.2
Area 2				
Alexander	492.4	573.0	479.7	633.4
Burke	434.7	487.7	411.5	577.9
Caldwell	521.8	550.6	522.8	633.0
McDowell	476.8	538.8	473.2	553.3
Wilkes	522.5	594.6	545.3	665.6
Tennessee				
Metropolitan Area C				
Hamilton	491.9	447.0	320.9	389.4
Metropolitan Area D				
Anderson	524.5	542.7	501.3	584.8
Blount	456.1	525.5	508.4	569.7
Knox	471.7	437.4	335.8	406.1
Area 7				
Bledsoe	590.9	703.1	590.9	657.8
Cumberland	608.7	656.6	567.9	663.4
Fentress	553.1	734.9	653.9	698.0
Grundy	609.5	663.6	555.8	658.9
Marion	608.1	628.5	508.6	597.5
Morgan	599.1	708.9	557.1	719.8
Scott	490.4	720.0	590.6	709.7
Sequatchie	547.1	711.1	611.0	588.7
Van Buren	589.1	747.1	593.5	640.2
Area 8a				
Bradley	497.5	515.0	464.0	529.8
Campbell	485.2	620.6	552.2	625.9
Loudon	474.4	517.1	422.1	524.2
McMinn	502.3	518.6	433.5	524.4
Meigs	498.4	680.2	604.4	680.4
Monroe	500.0	644.7	560.6	603.7
Polk	505.6	610.5	545.8	649.5
Rhea	532.7	544.2	501.8	555.3
Roane	503.0	553.7	463.7	577.5
Sevier	482.7	522.4	547.8	614.6
Union	558.1	606.4	545.1	634.9

TABLE 2 *(continued)*

Area	1960	1950	1940	1930
Area 8b				
Carter	454.7	519.0	487.1	559.2
Claiborne	492.2	583.1	535.7	659.3
Cocke	551.5	568.8	511.0	616.0
Grainger	509.1	544.1	523.0	577.0
Greene	449.5	508.9	444.9	554.1
Hamblen	498.6	499.2	389.2	420.6
Hancock	562.0	609.1	567.0	692.3
Hawkins	501.8	543.3	499.4	557.7
Jefferson	435.0	439.0	443.2	527.1
Johnson	467.7	594.8	547.4	595.2
Sullivan	459.8	476.6	415.1	480.4
Unicoi	515.3	536.7	472.7	626.0
Washington	467.8	478.1	377.8	466.6
Virginia				
Metropolitan Area A				
Roanoke	469.7	404.0	267.9	396.6
Area 1				
Buchanan	708.3	766.1	767.1	824.5
Dickenson	633.4	758.1	700.5	843.0
Lee	523.3	621.9	599.7	691.6
Tazewell	532.2	597.6	547.2	663.5
Wise	548.1	613.3	530.4	667.0
Area 2				
Bland	492.9	605.7	482.1	676.6
Carroll	467.6	552.4	505.9	647.8
Grayson	461.2	491.4	459.2	547.3
Russell	565.8	625.7	574.9	692.6
Scott	483.0	566.2	510.8	606.0
Smyth	467.4	513.5	489.9	606.3
Washington	464.7	492.0	460.6	546.3
Wythe	455.7	528.4	464.6	614.0
Area 3				
Alleghany	498.0	460.0	362.8	487.5
Bath	517.1	513.4	462.0	569.9
Botetourt	531.4	531.4	447.2	540.1
Craig	580.3	583.5	421.0	551.1
Floyd	461.4	524.1	479.3	563.1
Giles	447.4	570.0	492.3	644.9
Highland	581.8	512.0	523.0	537.9
Montgomery	435.1	437.9	403.0	532.3
Pulaski	454.8	516.7	451.0	577.0
Rockbridge	505.9	490.8	421.1	583.6

TABLE 2 *(continued)*

Area	1960	1950	1940	1930
Area 4				
Augusta	488.5	449.2	367.7	441.5
Clarke	522.2	509.5	405.6	449.0
Frederick	522.8	466.5	343.5	453.0
Page	490.9	494.1	436.1	542.7
Rockingham	451.6	450.5	382.3	492.1
Shenandoah	496.2	490.1	402.6	479.4
Warren	467.1	490.0	413.6	525.9
West Virginia				
Metropolitan Area B				
Cabell	443.5	413.1	328.2	416.0
Wayne	553.0	583.8	539.5	670.8
Metropolitan Area C				
Kanawha	512.1	498.7	405.2	515.2
Fayette	528.1	591.4	516.8	677.1
Area 2b				
Braxton	571.4	590.0	524.2	647.6
Calhoun	542.2	615.9	582.3	660.9
Clay	650.0	722.5	670.4	804.2
Doddridge	563.4	579.7	455.2	542.8
Gilmer	495.5	526.8	538.9	561.7
Lewis	447.1	454.2	384.3	410.8
Nicholas	579.7	650.4	539.8	665.2
Ritchie	568.3	547.1	424.5	550.7
Roane	495.0	545.6	466.9	575.3
Upshur	487.2	551.5	444.7	515.6
Webster	697.6	701.7	627.9	731.0
Wirt	567.8	541.4	533.2	618.5
Area 3				
Barbour	487.3	563.3	475.6	591.4
Harrison	474.9	461.4	360.3	474.5
Marion	426.5	435.6	369.8	500.4
Monongalia	438.0	457.7	390.1	556.9
Preston	617.0	614.7	509.7	589.6
Taylor	501.3	507.0	383.6	520.2
Area 4				
Boone	552.7	681.3	598.7	763.4
Logan	583.5	672.6	574.4	764.3
McDowell	573.1	651.5	575.6	758.9
Mercer	461.3	500.5	410.4	544.6
Mingo	626.0	702.9	554.1	682.1
Raleigh	501.7	575.8	541.9	723.2
Wyoming	605.1	703.7	609.8	747.0

TABLE 2 *(continued)*

Area	1960	1950	1940	1930
Area 5				
Grant	538.9	618.3	490.4	577.8
Greenbrier	543.2	553.5	496.2	608.6
Hampshire	506.5	554.4	464.7	579.7
Hardy	537.2	576.4	502.5	620.6
Mineral	479.5	490.0	401.9	504.3
Monroe	486.9	559.4	433.8	556.2
Pendleton	541.2	547.6	552.3	657.6
Pocahontas	501.4	578.3	499.3	595.5
Randolph	518.6	562.6	516.4	578.1
Summers	466.9	514.8	463.9	511.9
Tucker	506.7	548.2	518.5	641.8
Area 6				
Berkeley	531.8	456.5	341.0	407.1
Jefferson	476.2	531.0	450.5	520.5
Morgan	554.5	545.7	462.3	555.0

TABLE 3

General Fertility Rates for the White Population of the United States, the Southern Appalachian Region, and Southern Appalachian Region Counties, 1960, 1950, 1940, and 1930[a]

Area	1960	1950	1940	1930
United States	113.9	102.3	78	86
Southern Appalachian Region, Total	111.0	124.8	127.4	135.7
Alabama				
Area 2				
Blount	105.5	115.9	127.4	172.9
Cullman	107.7	118.4	126.1	148.0
DeKalb	108.0	114.3	115.9	169.8
Jackson	127.6	141.6	149.5	164.6
Marshall	126.1	129.8	104.3	131.9
Georgia				
Metropolitan Area A				
Walker	108.6	115.3	117.0	127.4
Area 1				
Bartow	119.6	128.6	122.0	93.3
Catoosa	105.8	111.8	92.9	113.7
Chattooga	114.7	117.4	129.2	141.3
Dade	125.3	153.3	158.5	201.5
Floyd	98.2	93.0	106.4	109.6
Gordon	109.9	110.5	124.9	135.7
Murray	89.9	139.5	138.4	153.3
Polk	114.1	109.2	109.7	117.4
Whitfield	116.4	117.5	115.1	147.6
Area 2				
Dawson	106.0	126.1	172.5	164.9
Fannin	89.8	127.2	140.7	188.0
Gilmer	83.1	139.4	150.7	184.4
Habersham	115.5	116.7	123.6	133.2
Lumpkin	110.6	122.8	127.2	139.4
Pickens	146.4	152.4	120.6	126.1
Rabun	113.0	137.7	174.7	132.4
Towns	79.3	111.7	127.3	171.6
Union	95.9	124.8	148.3	163.2
White	121.1	145.7	147.5	173.4
Kentucky				
Metropolitan Area C				
Boyd	106.1	116.7	102.2	111.2

[a] Based on average annual births for the periods 1929-1931, 1939-1941, 1949-1951, and 1959-1960, adjusted for underregistration.

Appendix A

TABLE 3 *(continued)*

Area	1960	1950	1940	1930
Area 8				
Carter	131.7	147.0	154.9	152.8
Clay	171.5	179.3	187.8	201.0
Elliott	129.4	170.9	173.8	242.4
Estill	124.1	127.2	129.5	146.0
Greenup	119.1	137.3	125.4	131.0
Jackson	127.6	152.8	149.1	161.8
Laurel	131.6	144.3	126.5	126.0
Lawrence	134.7	138.0	132.8	142.2
Lee	157.7	184.0	126.5	147.4
Lewis	143.2	171.0	151.1	168.1
Magoffin	148.5	214.8	198.3	194.9
Menifee	146.2	164.0	165.8	166.4
Morgan	147.5	153.4	154.7	194.3
Owsley	145.0	185.2	196.6	238.6
Powell	145.9	156.1	139.3	161.6
Rowan	105.0	125.0	152.8	171.1
Wolfe	182.7	163.2	164.9	137.8
Area 9				
Bell	131.8	160.5	148.0	124.9
Breathitt	167.8	160.2	178.1	174.7
Floyd	139.9	170.6	156.2	160.7
Harlan	136.1	158.1	146.9	169.7
Johnson	118.6	144.3	146.6	151.0
Knott	123.6	166.4	177.6	213.1
Knox	129.3	136.9	144.1	154.8
Leslie	235.3	200.5	182.8	198.3
Letcher	141.8	167.8	165.0	161.0
McCreary	151.2	157.9	177.6	129.8
Martin	158.0	190.6	176.6	170.9
Perry	161.3	186.3	165.4	214.2
Pike	130.1	169.2	165.3	185.6
Whitley	115.5	125.7	136.1	169.9
North Carolina				
Metropolitan Area A				
Buncombe	97.1	92.7	90.8	90.6
Area 1				
Alleghany	100.3	103.8	110.3	128.2
Ashe	116.2	136.5	132.8	157.2
Avery	114.1	130.1	164.2	177.9
Cherokee	98.0	130.5	156.9	138.1
Clay	128.2	128.9	165.8	190.8
Graham	120.4	147.8	182.0	157.4

TABLE 3 *(continued)*

Area	1960	1950	1940	1930
Haywood	107.6	115.9	127.7	149.5
Henderson	101.0	120.6	112.7	121.1
Jackson	96.3	125.2	131.4	143.9
Macon	97.6	121.5	143.3	160.0
Madison	89.3	101.7	130.8	152.1
Mitchell	107.2	123.9	133.4	164.1
Swain	117.7	121.3	164.4	141.2
Transylvania	114.1	144.8	157.5	158.5
Watauga	90.2	116.8	126.4	149.9
Yancey	99.8	123.1	133.5	134.9
Area 2				
Alexander	105.2	125.3	139.1	159.1
Burke	93.0	104.6	115.7	130.9
Caldwell	121.2	131.1	142.7	157.4
McDowell	117.3	129.5	125.8	142.3
Wilkes	112.2	127.2	142.5	177.6
Tennessee				
Metropolitan Area C				
Hamilton	105.5	103.5	102.8	67.6
Metropolitan Area D				
Anderson	110.6	120.1	121.6	139.9
Blount	97.1	117.7	136.1	133.1
Knox	102.1	97.5	90.7	70.9
Area 7				
Bledsoe	132.9	159.6	161.5	117.6
Cumberland	135.8	142.6	125.8	133.7
Fentress	140.9	158.8	206.0	188.0
Grundy	136.9	143.1	141.5	122.0
Marion	122.5	139.3	157.0	135.5
Morgan	112.0	133.5	147.6	183.7
Scott	109.1	160.8	255.6	266.5
Sequatchie	97.4	123.7	142.7	132.1
Van Buren	134.1	130.2	170.2	241.8
Area 8a				
Bradley	111.4	142.4	118.7	132.6
Campbell	112.8	135.4	166.4	161.2
Loudon	102.3	109.7	110.6	124.2
McMinn	105.9	114.0	112.8	131.8
Meigs	106.9	155.5	149.2	127.9
Monroe	116.6	141.9	158.6	145.7
Polk	117.9	140.4	130.2	194.4
Rhea	121.0	125.7	141.2	104.7
Roane	106.0	127.6	123.5	143.5

TABLE 3 *(continued)*

Area	1960	1950	1940	1930
Sevier	101.4	114.8	140.9	154.7
Union	108.5	143.3	253.0	246.0
Area 8b				
Carter	87.8	105.0	125.5	136.1
Claiborne	110.1	122.3	156.5	120.7
Cocke	118.8	135.7	128.1	154.5
Grainger	116.3	118.1	130.5	121.1
Greene	96.6	107.2	104.0	118.2
Hamblen	96.1	115.2	104.7	100.2
Hancock	120.8	133.7	159.2	209.0
Hawkins	108.2	124.6	134.2	150.3
Jefferson	94.8	101.1	135.5	134.7
Johnson	94.4	124.3	157.6	167.7
Sullivan	96.1	108.1	108.3	84.4
Unicoi	111.7	113.8	110.6	115.0
Washington	113.6	112.4	108.3	102.8
Virginia				
Metropolitan Area A				
Roanoke	95.3	92.8	83.6	92.8
Area 1				
Buchanan	151.4	170.4	198.5	229.3
Dickenson	130.7	162.8	175.4	194.5
Lee	104.5	134.7	138.6	159.0
Tazewell	123.9	157.8	162.3	178.3
Wise	123.5	144.4	136.0	160.3
Area 2				
Bland	87.7	115.5	121.9	146.9
Carroll	93.5	105.0	106.2	145.4
Grayson	102.6	120.3	113.8	131.1
Russell	114.5	143.7	148.8	169.3
Scott	102.1	116.4	136.4	159.3
Smyth	104.4	109.5	126.4	161.0
Washington	101.2	118.3	123.2	127.6
Wythe	96.0	127.2	99.7	154.2
Area 3				
Alleghany	107.3	117.3	90.0	103.0
Bath	112.2	103.1	108.5	93.9
Botetourt	99.2	102.7	108.8	118.0
Craig	105.4	111.1	92.7	107.7
Floyd	96.8	103.5	117.6	130.2
Giles	90.8	128.9	135.0	167.8
Highland	109.7	103.7	152.0	140.1
Montgomery	103.8	109.9	107.6	113.0

TABLE 3 *(continued)*

Area	1960	1950	1940	1930
Pulaski	95.6	113.2	116.1	127.7
Rockbridge	126.3	115.0	104.8	123.2
Area 4				
Augusta	100.8	98.2	95.6	96.5
Clarke	112.6	121.2	127.9	110.9
Frederick	89.2	106.0	98.4	116.4
Page	105.7	116.2	113.1	145.3
Rockingham	97.9	102.3	102.7	115.6
Shenandoah	99.7	104.2	101.7	117.2
Warren	102.5	112.5	115.1	121.9
West Virginia				
Metropolitan Area B				
Cabell	103.1	105.3	91.0	89.6
Wayne	106.0	116.8	128.0	140.3
Metropolitan Area C				
Kanawha	110.0	120.4	135.7	123.2
Fayette	109.9	130.5	126.6	155.5
Area 2b				
Braxton	127.3	138.4	123.3	136.4
Calhoun	112.2	117.6	136.3	153.0
Clay	149.5	182.4	156.4	162.0
Doddridge	112.8	97.0	106.0	139.7
Gilmer	113.3	98.4	119.0	128.8
Lewis	103.5	99.1	81.8	93.6
Nicholas	119.9	147.5	125.4	164.3
Ritchie	114.3	112.2	99.9	117.0
Roane	95.1	110.9	104.7	129.4
Upshur	107.9	125.8	108.3	121.8
Webster	129.5	141.1	140.1	156.0
Wirt	118.3	102.9	111.5	113.5
Area 3				
Barbour	106.5	115.8	136.0	147.7
Harrison	103.5	103.8	91.3	110.1
Marion	93.7	103.1	97.3	109.4
Monongalia	97.2	105.3	93.1	128.7
Preston	128.6	128.9	125.9	143.0
Taylor	102.0	109.8	94.2	114.3
Area 4				
Boone	115.4	149.6	151.6	181.7
Logan	124.6	159.1	150.8	180.3
McDowell	133.0	170.0	183.0	183.0
Mercer	104.2	116.4	130.8	139.0
Mingo	144.8	177.7	160.9	148.0

Appendix A

TABLE 3 *(continued)*

Area	1960	1950	1940	1930
Raleigh	108.7	127.4	160.2	189.7
Wyoming	120.3	161.7	187.3	182.5
Area 5				
Grant	133.3	141.6	157.4	144.7
Greenbrier	117.6	135.9	124.2	145.4
Hampshire	101.5	109.8	114.6	134.9
Hardy	120.0	114.6	125.5	144.7
Mineral	103.7	116.8	104.2	104.5
Monroe	94.3	117.1	104.9	111.1
Pendleton	111.5	129.3	143.2	157.6
Pocahontas	130.5	150.1	125.0	133.2
Randolph	128.6	128.6	137.8	139.9
Summers	96.6	115.1	110.2	117.7
Tucker	125.4	123.0	109.5	130.3
Area 6				
Berkeley	113.5	105.8	80.2	102.6
Jefferson	105.7	117.5	128.8	132.1
Morgan	121.2	139.0	110.0	134.8

TABLE 4

Standardized General Fertility Rates for the White Population of the United States, the Southern Appalachian Region, and Southern Appalachian Region Counties, 1960, 1950, 1940, and 1930[a]

Area	1960	1950	1940	1930
United States	118.9	102.3	80.6	84.7
Southern Appalachian Region, Total	117.8	122.9	122.0	129.5
Alabama				
Area 2				
Blount	115.2	119.2	121.3	163.2
Cullman	116.9	118.7	120.1	142.1
DeKalb	117.0	117.4	111.3	159.9
Jackson	135.6	144.5	140.6	157.4
Marshall	132.5	131.4	98.5	124.7
Georgia				
Metropolitan Area A				
Walker	113.2	113.9	111.4	121.7
Area 1				
Bartow	128.6	128.3	114.8	90.4
Catoosa	105.4	109.6	88.4	110.8
Chattooga	124.0	114.0	116.4	133.4
Dade	124.6	150.3	157.9	205.4
Floyd	103.3	93.5	97.6	102.2
Gordon	114.6	111.4	117.6	130.1
Murray	92.8	138.8	130.9	147.4
Polk	124.3	110.4	102.6	108.9
Whitfield	120.2	116.4	107.2	139.1
Area 2				
Dawson	109.7	126.6	163.5	157.5
Fannin	98.6	123.8	137.1	181.4
Gilmer	88.8	138.6	140.8	176.2
Habersham	120.1	113.0	120.0	128.5
Lumpkin	111.3	123.1	122.5	138.9
Pickens	147.8	159.3	119.2	120.1
Rabun	119.7	140.7	170.1	125.7
Towns	88.9	111.6	122.7	171.3
Union	106.0	127.1	145.5	153.3
White	125.0	147.2	143.9	172.0

[a] Indirectly standardized using five-year age-specific birth rates for United States native white women, 1950.

TABLE 4 *(continued)*

Area	1960	1950	1940	1930
Kentucky				
Metropolitan Area C				
Boyd	111.7	115.4	99.0	103.7
Area 8				
Carter	139.1	149.0	149.0	151.2
Clay	178.3	176.2	180.8	196.0
Elliott	133.3	175.3	165.7	236.7
Estill	131.5	132.1	130.7	141.6
Greenup	121.9	134.4	122.2	128.7
Jackson	143.1	153.4	143.3	160.9
Laurel	142.4	143.4	123.6	125.3
Lawrence	146.8	144.8	130.0	141.4
Lee	168.6	186.8	125.9	148.6
Lewis	151.4	172.5	145.2	168.0
Magoffin	158.5	207.8	188.2	189.4
Menifee	157.7	164.0	168.5	169.5
Morgan	157.5	156.7	149.8	192.7
Owsley	155.9	188.9	192.3	232.5
Powell	151.0	156.6	134.3	161.8
Rowan	104.2	122.1	147.0	164.9
Wolfe	201.7	171.7	160.0	136.2
Area 9				
Bell	144.2	154.0	144.4	117.6
Breathitt	176.6	163.1	170.9	164.3
Floyd	151.1	164.0	147.0	149.1
Harlan	150.3	153.0	138.0	152.3
Johnson	126.7	144.1	138.6	143.7
Knott	133.1	162.2	168.4	201.7
Knox	143.9	137.1	142.1	149.3
Leslie	238.2	195.2	176.9	189.3
Letcher	153.5	163.3	155.1	148.0
McCreary	169.4	159.2	173.1	121.1
Martin	164.7	181.7	174.0	168.0
Perry	170.8	178.7	158.3	194.8
Pike	137.1	160.2	158.8	172.2
Whitley	129.8	128.4	134.7	163.9
North Carolina				
Metropolitan Area A				
Buncombe	104.6	91.8	86.7	87.1
Area 1				
Alleghany	105.5	106.1	108.6	126.4
Ashe	121.8	139.9	130.1	153.0
Avery	120.8	129.7	157.8	173.8

TABLE 4 *(continued)*

Area	1960	1950	1940	1930
Cherokee	108.6	131.3	150.4	134.2
Clay	149.7	129.2	160.9	192.0
Graham	129.9	150.2	172.3	149.8
Haywood	112.1	112.2	122.2	143.0
Henderson	108.8	122.3	109.0	119.5
Jackson	100.7	126.1	127.5	139.2
Macon	105.6	125.6	138.4	156.3
Madison	97.3	102.3	126.2	148.8
Mitchell	114.1	125.2	125.7	157.8
Swain	127.6	127.9	160.1	135.1
Transylvania	119.1	142.8	147.7	150.5
Watauga	91.8	114.0	121.8	147.6
Yancey	108.3	122.1	127.4	130.8
Area 2				
Alexander	110.4	125.3	137.0	158.6
Burke	97.6	103.7	107.3	125.5
Caldwell	123.3	128.5	132.3	150.1
McDowell	122.0	127.4	118.6	134.2
Wilkes	117.7	125.8	134.2	175.3
Tennessee				
Metropolitan Area C				
Hamilton	109.5	102.1	99.5	63.4
Metropolitan Area D				
Anderson	120.1	114.4	115.8	134.5
Blount	105.4	114.3	127.7	126.5
Knox	107.0	95.2	87.7	66.4
Area 7				
Bledsoe	139.2	163.2	155.4	114.5
Cumberland	142.8	148.2	119.6	129.5
Fentress	152.4	159.9	195.7	180.0
Grundy	145.7	143.7	139.5	117.6
Marion	126.5	145.0	153.5	127.6
Morgan	122.6	135.7	144.7	179.3
Scott	107.8	160.7	247.5	258.9
Sequatchie	102.5	122.7	138.2	128.1
Van Buren	141.2	132.3	166.3	230.4
Area 8a				
Bradley	113.6	140.7	111.2	126.9
Campbell	122.6	134.5	157.8	155.0
Loudon	108.6	109.8	105.6	119.2
McMinn	111.2	114.0	110.2	126.8
Meigs	121.9	158.1	140.9	123.4
Monroe	125.4	140.6	153.3	141.9

TABLE 4 *(continued)*

Area	1960	1950	1940	1930
Polk	126.5	139.7	125.0	186.0
Rhea	129.3	126.2	133.5	103.4
Roane	111.9	124.5	119.0	137.3
Sevier	103.3	115.0	136.3	149.4
Union	113.1	141.7	251.6	242.1
Area 8b				
Carter	93.3	104.5	116.3	127.2
Claiborne	116.4	122.6	152.8	115.5
Cocke	121.6	136.3	121.6	150.9
Grainger	120.7	121.4	126.8	120.2
Greene	98.7	106.1	100.0	113.1
Hamblen	95.4	112.6	100.0	97.5
Hancock	128.9	132.7	155.0	200.9
Hawkins	113.7	126.6	129.5	144.8
Jefferson	93.7	100.3	130.0	130.2
Johnson	102.8	126.4	154.4	162.5
Sullivan	100.3	102.8	100.2	77.9
Unicoi	120.4	110.2	107.9	109.9
Washington	118.6	107.9	105.0	95.7
Virginia				
Metropolitan Area A				
Roanoke	100.4	91.7	82.7	85.8
Area 1				
Buchanan	152.5	160.6	184.9	220.8
Dickenson	139.0	157.7	166.4	187.8
Lee	118.0	136.1	132.5	152.6
Tazewell	132.6	155.5	151.8	167.9
Wise	132.6	139.7	131.5	153.4
Area 2				
Bland	93.3	114.1	125.5	139.9
Carroll	99.5	105.8	103.8	142.0
Grayson	109.4	121.5	109.6	127.3
Russell	120.8	142.3	142.5	166.1
Scott	109.4	115.3	130.8	156.3
Smyth	109.8	107.5	120.7	156.2
Washington	105.9	118.2	118.9	122.8
Wythe	104.8	126.0	95.3	149.3
Area 3				
Alleghany	115.9	118.8	84.3	96.6
Bath	116.3	110.2	106.2	87.3
Botetourt	104.9	105.8	108.3	118.6
Craig	111.1	113.9	97.1	107.2
Floyd	106.6	110.0	114.1	133.7

TABLE 4 *(continued)*

Area	1960	1950	1940	1930
Giles	103.0	122.1	126.3	164.1
Highland	116.7	116.6	147.0	135.6
Montgomery	102.8	103.5	103.7	108.7
Pulaski	104.9	112.1	107.6	121.5
Rockbridge	131.2	112.4	102.0	120.5
Area 4				
Augusta	106.6	97.7	91.2	93.8
Clarke	118.9	125.7	126.5	112.0
Frederick	93.0	104.0	94.5	112.9
Page	113.2	118.7	113.8	143.8
Rockingham	99.5	98.2	100.0	112.6
Shenandoah	106.1	108.0	104.0	116.5
Warren	113.5	113.6	107.2	119.6
West Virginia				
Metropolitan Area B				
Cabell	109.4	102.4	89.3	86.0
Wayne	112.2	115.7	124.8	135.2
Metropolitan Area C				
Kanawha	116.5	115.9	127.2	115.4
Fayette	124.1	128.2	118.9	146.5
Area 2b				
Braxton	140.9	146.1	119.6	137.1
Calhoun	124.8	122.8	129.7	148.6
Clay	161.9	179.2	151.3	151.6
Doddridge	129.9	100.9	103.6	142.5
Gilmer	113.3	98.4	119.0	128.8
Lewis	103.5	99.1	81.8	93.6
Nicholas	119.9	147.5	125.4	164.3
Ritchie	114.3	112.2	99.9	117.0
Roane	95.1	110.9	104.7	129.4
Upshur	107.9	125.8	108.3	121.8
Webster	129.5	141.1	140.1	156.0
Wirt	118.3	102.9	111.5	113.5
Area 3				
Barbour	106.5	115.8	136.0	147.7
Harrison	103.5	103.8	91.3	110.1
Marion	93.7	103.1	79.3	109.4
Monongalia	97.2	105.3	93.1	128.7
Preston	128.6	128.9	125.9	143.0
Taylor	102.0	109.8	94.2	114.3
Area 4				
Boone	115.4	149.6	151.6	181.7
Logan	124.6	159.1	150.8	180.3

TABLE 4 *(continued)*

Area	1960	1950	1940	1930
McDowell	133.0	170.0	183.0	183.0
Mercer	104.2	116.4	130.8	139.0
Mingo	144.8	177.7	160.9	148.0
Raleigh	108.7	127.4	160.2	189.7
Wyoming	120.3	161.7	187.3	182.5
Area 5				
Grant	133.3	141.6	157.4	144.7
Greenbrier	117.6	135.9	124.2	145.4
Hampshire	101.5	109.8	114.6	134.9
Hardy	120.0	114.6	125.5	144.7
Mineral	103.7	116.8	104.2	104.5
Monroe	94.3	117.1	104.9	111.1
Pendleton	111.5	129.3	143.2	157.6
Pocahontas	130.5	150.1	125.0	133.2
Randolph	128.6	128.6	137.8	139.9
Summers	96.6	115.1	110.2	117.7
Tucker	125.4	123.0	109.5	130.3
Area 6				
Berkeley	113.5	105.8	80.2	102.6
Jefferson	105.7	117.5	128.8	132.1
Morgan	121.2	139.0	110.0	134.8

Appendix B

SOURCE OF DATA

1. Sixteenth Census of the United States: 1940. Vol. II, *Characteristics of the Population*, Parts 1, 2, 3, 5, 6, 7, Table 22.

2. United States Census of Population: 1950. Vol. II, *Characteristics of the Population*, P-B1, 11, 17, 33, 42, 48, Table 41, and U.S. Summary, Table 39.

3. United States Census of Population: 1960. *General Population Characteristics*, PC(1)-1B, 2B, 12B, 19B, 35B, 44B, 50B, Tables 27 and 46.

4. United States Bureau of Census, *Births, Stillbirths, and Infant Mortality Statistics*, 1929, 1930, 1931, Table I.

5. United States Bureau of the Census, *Vital Statistics of the United States*, Supplement, 1939-40, Part III, Table 1.

6. United States Bureau of the Census, *Vital Statistics of the United States*, 1941, Part II, Table II.

7. National Office of Vital Statistics, *Vital Statistics of the United States*, 1949, Part II, Table 1.

8. National Office of Vital Statistics, *Vital Statistics of the United States*, 1950, Vol. II, Table 13.

9. National Office of Vital Statistics, *Vital Statistics of the United States*, 1951, Vol. I, Table 17.

10. National Office of Vital Statistics, *Vital Statistics of the United States*, 1959, Vol. I, Section II, Table 25.

11. James S. Brown and K. M. George, "Components of Population Change, Southern Appalachians, 1940-50 and 1950-60: Estimates of Net Migration and Natural Increase for Each Metropolitan Area, State Economic Area, and County," University of Kentucky Department of Rural Sociology (unpublished data).

12. United States Bureau of Census, *Historical Statistics of the United States, Colonial Times to 1957*, 1960, Table B 19-30.

13. United States Bureau of the Census, *Statistical Abstract of the United States*, 1961, Table 43.

14. North Carolina State Board of Health, *Annual Report of Public Health Statistics Section,* 1960, Part II, Raleigh, N.C., Table 3.

15. Tennessee Department of Public Health, *Tennessee Vital Statistics,* 1960, Nashville, Tenn., Table 10.

16. Virginia State Department of Health, *Statistical Annual Report,* 1960, Richmond, Va., Table 7.

17. Published 1960 birth data furnished by the Alabama, Georgia, Kentucky, and West Virginia Departments of Health.

Index

Age: relation to fertility, 90
Age at marriage: 68
Alabama: 9, 19-20
Allegheny Plateau: migration from, 52; population decline in, 11-12
Appalachia: definition of, 1, 19-20; interest in, 1; population of, 10, 21
Asheville, N. C.: 49
Attitudes: 74-75
Attitude change: and population-economy imbalance, 107
Augusta County, Va.: 49

Beebe, Gilbert W.: 32, 85
Belcher, John C.: 37, 38
Berkeley County, W. Va.: 48
Birth control practices: acceptance of, 32-33; comparative data on disapproval, 87; compared to underdeveloped nations, 85; opinion concerning, 31, 86-87
Birth rates: balance with death rates, 64-65; correlates of, 68; standardization of, 35. See also Fertility
Births: attributable to out-migrants, 62-63; underregistration of, 34
Black Mountains: 9
Blue Ridge Mountains: migration from, 53; population change in, 12
Bowles, Gladys K.: 55
Bristol, Va.: 47
Brown, James S.: 57

Caudill, Harry: 1
Census, U.S.: 133-34
Chattanooga, Tenn.: 47, 49
Child-rearing: cost of, 68
Coal regions: population decline in, 11-12

County fertility types: definition, 61; effect of migration, 73; links to fertility attitudes, 72; residence pattern, 65-68
Crude birth rate: correlation with net migration, 57-60; definition of, 33; region and county data, 109-14. See also Fertility rate
Cumberland Plateau: high fertility in, 48; migration from, 53; population decline in, 11-12

Deaths: significance for region population trends, 3
Demographic factors: in fertility decline, 6-7, 101-102
Depression, Great: 31
Development: motivational base for policy, 107; strategies for, 105
Differential fertility: factors in, 88-92 passim; and religious fundamentalism, 103

Ecological correlations: of fertility decline, 71
Economic factors: 1, 2
Economy: imbalance with population, 106
Education: correlate of low achievement, 95-98; proportion functionally illiterate, 18; regional-national comparisons, 17-18; relation to fertility, 89-90; schooling completed, 18, 23
Estill County, Ky.: 48

Family system: consequences for fertility, 68; patriarchal, 68; role of the woman in, 90-91
Fertility: comparison of measures, 35-37; correlate of economic status, 77; geographic distribu-

Fertility (*continued*):
tion of rates, 39-46; link between high fertility and poverty, 106; measures of, 33-34; regional-national comparisons, 35-46; trends in, 35-36. *See also* Births and Birth rates

Fertility decline: and age structure, 37; ecology of, 38, 43-46; period of rapid, 50

Fertility differential: rural-urban, 64-69

Fertility ratio: correlation with net migration, 57-60; definition, 32-33; region and county data, 115-20

General fertility rate: correlation with net migration, 57-60; definition, 32-33; region and county data, 121-26. *See also* Fertility

George, K. M.: 57

Georgia: 9, 19-20

Glynn, Jerome: 54

Goldberg, David: 98-99

Great Smoky Mountains: 9

Great Valley: economic development in, 50; low fertility in, 50; migration from, 53; population change in, 12

Growth of the American Family Study: 72

Guttman scale: of religious fundamentalism, 93

Hamilton County, Tenn.: 47

Human resources: development emphasis, 105

Ideal age at marriage: for a man and for a woman, 82-84; relation to county fertility type, 83-84

Ideal family size: and actual family size, 72-73; comparison to other studies, 76-77; economically not well-off couple, 80-81; economically well-off couple, 79-80; and perceived economic status, 77-82

Income, family: change in, 29-30;

Income, family (*continued*):
national comparison, 30; poverty level, 29

Indianapolis Study: 4; criticism of theory in, 5

Industrial development: changing birth and death rates, 63-64

Industrial structure: changes in, 24-26; regional and national comparisons, 24-25

Jefferson County, W. Va.: 48

Jehlik, Paul J.: 54

Kentucky: 9, 19-20; Eastern: high fertility, 38, 48, 50-51; migration from, 53; population decline in, 11-12

Knox County, Tenn.: 47

Knoxville, Tenn.: 47, 49

Labor force: females in, 23; regional-national comparisons, 23

Leslie County, Ky.: migration from, 53; high fertility in, 31, 50-51

Life cycle: population change by, 15; population composition by, 14-15; regional-national comparisons, 14-15

Logan County, W. Va.: 32

Magoffin County, Ky.: 50

Malthusian thesis: 3

Mangalam, Joseph J.: 57

Marion County, W. Va.: 50

Marital status: by sex, 16; regional-national comparisons, 16-17

Methodology: alternative approaches to study of migration, 56; problems in calculating number of births attributable to out-migrants, 62-63; relation of personal and social characteristics to attitudes and fertility change, 93-95

Metropolitan areas: lower fertility in, 63-64

Migration: age selectivity in, 55; attitude similarity to, 98-99; changing attitudes toward, 7-8;

Migration (*continued*):
definitions of, 55-56; extent of out-migration, 52; relationship to fertility attitudes, 105; selectivity of young women, 55; sociological perspective of, 56-57; strategy in population-economy imbalance, 106
Migration systems: 7-8
Monongahela Valley: 50
Monongalia County, W. Va.: 50
Morgan County, W. Va.: 48

Nagel, Ernest: 70
Negroes: *See* Nonwhite population
New York: 9, 19-20
Nonwhite population: regional-national comparison, 13; trends in, 13-14
North Carolina: 9, 19-20

Occupational structure: changes in, 27-28; regional and national comparisons, 27-28
Owsley County, Ky.: 48

Parent's family size: relation to fertility, 90
Physiographic divisions: migration from, 53
Population growth: regional-national comparisons, 10; regional trends, 10-11, 21
Poverty: link with high fertility, 106. *See also* Income
Princeton Study: 4, 5-6

Rainwater, Lee: 99
Religious affiliation: relation to fertility, 91-92
Religious fundamentalism: and fertility attitudes, 95-98, 99-100; in Southern Appalachian Region, 92; measure of, 93; theoretical relation to fertility, 92-93
Religiousness: church attendance as measure of, 92
Residential patterns: relation to fertility decline, 66-67
Resources: relation to high fertility, 32

Roanoke, Va.: 49
Rockingham County, Va.: 50
Roosevelt, Franklin D.: 31
Rural: background and fertility, 99; definition, 65; population, 12

Schwarzweller, Harry K.: 57
Sex: industrial structure by, 25-26; labor force by, 23; marital status by, 16; occupational structure by, 28
Sex roles: 23-24
Shenandoah Valley: 50
Social demography: areas of interest, 101-104 *passim;* type of issues in, 10
Socioeconomic status: correlate of low status, 95-98; index of, 89; relation to fertility, 88-89
Southern Appalachian Survey: 74
Standard Metropolitan Statistical Areas: county population change through migration, 51; definition, 65
Standardization: *See* Birth rates
Standardized general fertility rate: correlation with net migration, 57-60; region and county data, 127-32
State economic areas: 9
Sullivan County, Tenn.: 47

Tennessee: 9, 19-20, 47, 48, 50
Theory of Demographic Transition: dynamics of population growth, 3-4; stages of demographic change, 64-65
Theory of fertility decline: 5
Thomas, Dorothy S.: 55

Unemployment: 23
Union County, Tenn.: 48
Urban areas: lower fertility in, 63-64; population increase in, 12
Urbanization: lag, 12
Urban place: definition of, 65

Values: 74-75
Vance, Rupert B.: 69
Virginia: 9, 19-20, 48
Vital Statistics: 133-34

Wakeley, Ray E.: 54
Washington County, Va.: 47
West Virginia: 9, 19-20, 48, 50
White population: distribution, 13.
    See also Nonwhite population

Women: rural-urban fertility dif-
    ferential, 68
World War II: 48

Yaukey, David: 104